Loving Who Shows Up

A different way of being for a new future

The benefits to the individual, the community,
and the earth itself of living with compassion

Eric Dowsett

Permission to reprint part of an article by James Barrett entitled
"What Is Heart Intelligence," originally published February, 2001
was graciously granted by the author.

Permission to reprint the English translation of the poem "Ithaca"
by Constantine Cavafy was graciously granted
by Harcourt Trade Publishing.

Author photograph: Teresa Luttrell
Cover photograph: www.shutterstock.com

ISBN 978-0-9830907-4-8

www.ericdowsett.com

The time has come the walrus said ...

to change the world we live in.

Adapted from Alice Through The Looking Glass
by Lewis Carroll

Contents

Acknowledgements

Many people have helped along the way, whether they knew it or not, and to all of those I am deeply grateful.

I would like to thank Chris and Rebecca in Australia for creating the space and putting up with me as I wrote the first draft.

Nina Gettler, my very patient and understanding editor.

And you, the reader, for you are the main reason I wrote this book.

Foreword

If we are looking for a new future, then we should understand how that new future can be created.

My reason for writing this book, apart from the great personal benefits of attempting to order my thoughts and paint a coherent picture, was to assist all those who seek the new but are not sure where to place the first step.

If we are to believe the modern day prophets, we are in a time of great potential, of change so deep and powerful, so significant there is nothing in our history books to compare. We are the agents of change, the change must begin with us.

And if we choose not to believe the modern day prophets, not think about the potential for change that the times offer, then *Loving Who Shows Up* will still be of tremendous value to you, your family, community, the earth itself.

Applying the information in this book to your everyday life then is, as they say, a win-win situation.

Enjoy.

Introduction

Have you ever wondered where we came from? Where we are going?

Have you ever stopped to think why you are as you are? Do you believe you have freedom of choice, or do you think you are a victim of circumstance?

These are questions that have been asked throughout history, and it would appear that there is no single answer that satisfies everyone. Perhaps there is no answer. Many people seem to be content with their life, until their life is threatened. Perhaps the answer—if there is one—is different for each of us, an answer, after all, is relative to the consciousness of the person asking.

The exploration of the human mind studying itself is an amazing concept, a process naturally limited by the perceptions of the "individual mind" but it is all we have without laying the final responsibility at the feet of a god.

This book offers an assortment of psychology, science, spirituality, and plain, old common sense to not only help us see how we are creating our world, but what can be done to make it a better world. It is about the how and why, about the reality that we appear to find ourselves in at any given moment, and what we can do to change it. It is about our potential to create a very different reality than the one we currently find ourselves in.

Most people on the planet have the same goal— to be safe and happy. For some, the road to safety and happiness is a hard one. Even those who have gained the outward signs happiness—material wealth and security—are still caught in an inner search for peace. And yet, in spite of advances in the material world, there does not seem to be any great shift in humanity's understanding of itself over the centuries. It is obvious that there have been great advances in science, medicine, and technology, but the intrinsic nature of humanity appears unchanged. We still look for safety and happiness in the same old way.

This book is about change on a very fundamental level. It is much more than a mere add-on to the current way of thinking; it has the potential to turn current perceptions on their head. I am endeavoring to present a very different point of view on how any reality is created and how it is sustained. I am not just offering concepts, theories, and stories, but a self-help manual containing simple things that you can put into practice immediately—if you so choose.

But remember that this is about my journey and the understandings I have gotten along the way. If any of the information contained in this book makes sense to you, if any of it stirs long-lost memories, if any of it resonates with something deep inside you, you will know. Take what you need, make it your own personal knowing, and leave the rest behind—perhaps for another day.

Reality is relative to the observer so that it can be different for each and every one of us. This book is not about judging any of those realities as better or worse than any other. It is about exploring how and where they come from, why they manifest as they do, and what—if anything—

can be done to create a world where safety and happiness are readily available for everyone.

I hope to be able to navigate through the minefield of questions, answers, doubts, and at the end of the book leave each of us with a different sense of how things work so that we can make our own decisions. Decisions not based on hearsay but on a deeper understanding of the nature of reality.

It is not my intention to divide the world into various collections of beliefs, some being better, some worse than others, but to look at what created these cultural beliefs in the first place. Perhaps, when we can find another way of looking at where the picture we have of ourselves came from, we will be more empowered to change that picture.

If we look back across time, we see—if history tells the truth—the rise and fall, of various cultures, each having its moment of glory followed by its decline. Within major cultures, we see sub-cultures appearing and disappearing. Yet, no matter how important any of these unique cultures were, they were still products of what went before them. Arising out of their past, using the same building blocks of creation that were used to create the past, they were essentially just more of the same. There may well have been great cultural leaps, great advances in thinking and social conscience, but they were all based on the same worldview. A worldview of separation, of individuality, of polarization. A worldview that sought to control the external so that the individual could find safety and happiness. It is not the products of the worldview that I am questioning, but this worldview itself, the essence behind the creation of the many civilizations and cultures, of which we are still a part.

Here we are today still battling evil in its many forms and nothing has changed. In thousands of years, nothing has really changed. If we truly desire change, not just of a government, but of the current worldview, then there has to be fundamental changes in each and every one of us. We will need to change not just our minds, not just our hearts, but the very understanding of who we are and the part we have played in the past in creating and sustaining the worldview. This sounds like an awfully big task, and, if you contemplate eating all the pie at once you may feel daunted. But take a slice at a time, and the task is easy.

Various people have appeared throughout history and offered us an alternative path. Very few of those people were taken seriously for very long. Even those who achieved popular acclaim have had their words manipulated over time to serve what has passed as the collective good. Yet the words of the prophets, the saints, these messengers from god all fell on the ears of those still living in a creation built on this very different perception.

The ears that heard the words interpreted the words through their individual pasts. They could only understand the words based on their current worldview that was so limited, and the words were often misunderstood. Many times, words of wisdom were taken by leaders and manipulated—possibly with the best of intentions—to fit the worldview of the time.

I believe that had the collective taken to heart the words of these people, the current worldview would be very different now. Taken to heart. This, I think, is the key.

In our endeavors to understand and control the world around us, we have looked outside ourselves for the answer.

We have tried to understand who we are and our place in this world through religion or science, through faith or facts. Through intellectual exercises or acceptance of words spoken or written in the past. If you think the teachings of love and compassion are alive and well in the world today, if you are content with the way the world is going—not just your own, personal world, but everyone else's world as well—then this book may not be for you. If you feel that humanity is—and has been for some time now—heading toward another dark age, then read on. You may find that the way of being offered here holds a promise of a very different worldview.

I believe that as long as we are suffering under the illusion that the personality is who we are, then the truth may be out there, but it is not something we can ever truly grasp. People throughout the ages have tried to discover truth, but they have always found, that the truth cannot be known from within the personality. We may manage to get glimpses of what could be the truth, but we have nothing by which to measure our discoveries. Trying to see the bigger picture from within the confines of who you believe yourself to be can only be successful to the degree you can be objective about your own view of reality.

Throughout this book I will introduce the words and "knowings" of many others to give different—or similar— perspectives on issues raised in the book. You may have heard of these people, some may be new to you. I would like to say now though, that everything in this book is hearsay, second-hand information.

You may believe that some of the quotes I cite are indeed the truth. But I have learned that even though the words quoted here may be the words originally spoken, they are not necessarily the truth. In the telling, repeated over and over again, words, sayings, or stories from the past are accepted as the truth. No matter that the words may have been changed a little here and there. What we read today is often accepted as the truth. I hope to explain this later on in the book, I am only bringing this up now because I want to make it clear that what we may have accepted in the past as truth may not be a truth at all. A lie told often enough will eventually become the truth.

> "Do not consider it proof just because it is written
> in books, for a liar who will deceive with his tongue
> will not hesitate to do the same with his pen."
>
> Maimonides

I do not think that the majority of people who have ever set pen to paper have deliberately lied or intended to mislead, although some may have done so, of course. I think each of us tells the story as we see it—or would like to see it—from the perspective of our personal limitations and expectations. I am no different, and this is why I caution you to not take my words too seriously, to not imagine that they contain any truth simply because I have written them down.

All I can do is offer a way through life that is based on personal, direct knowing, not on the words of others, no matter who they are or may have been. I mean no disrespect. Many people have influenced my thinking in a multitude of ways. The words of others have often supported my worldview or expanded my ability to be more open to other worldviews.

To sort fact from fiction is not easily done. Knowing the difference could be the hardest part. And because it is the very foundation upon which we have based our lives, it will be brought into question and therefore perhaps needs to be looked at from a totally different perspective. To do this, we need to begin to question everything we have ever been told; everything that, until now, we have accepted as the truth. Because our parents told us, because society told us, because religion told us, because science told us, because history told us are no longer good enough reasons to accept without questioning what is really going on.

People have been questioning for millennia, perhaps trying to understand the meaning of life. Some may have found answers that satisfied them and supported the foundation of their beliefs. For the most part though, questions are only asked from within the framework of the current, limited understanding of the person asking the questions. Answers galore can be found there, but only answers to the questions being asked, and only answers that the current worldview of the individual can rationalize. These may or may not be answers to the big questions in life. More than likely, they are answers that satisfy the individual for a brief moment in time.

The Buddha was reported to have begun each discourse with the words "Thus have I heard" thereby not claiming the words as the truth. I do the same...

Whoever you perceive yourself to be—on any level subtle or gross—affects those around you, as they affect you. Whoever you perceive yourself to be affects the spaces that you inhabit—your home, your workplace, everywhere— just as those spaces affect you. And, whoever you perceive yourself to be, reacts whether consciously or not to those other people and to the spaces or environment around you.

Most of us are on automatic pilot, making decisions within subconscious limitations, decisions that add to and support the current worldview of right and wrong, good and bad, safe and unsafe. If you feel there has to be something more, if you want to change your life but don't know how, if you want to bring greater peace into your life, the lives of friends and family, and the world at large, then you may find some help in this book. If you want to understand the part you are playing in creating the worldview that is commonly accepted at the moment and do something about it, then you could well have picked up the right book.

Chapter One
Where Do We Come From?

From the early days in my life, I sensed a difference in myself to most people around me. This feeling was understood by my father. Perhaps this is common to all children—this feeling of being different and special that life has not yet taken from us.

Early childhood did not come equipped with the knowledge and wisdom to understand what this difference was, other than a young mind trying to understand itself. I would look around at the behavior of those around me and wonder at the way people treated each other. I was not able to reconcile much of what I saw with how I felt inside. Not having any understanding of what was happening or why, no one to whom I could turn and ask, this was a very alienating time for me. Even if there had been someone to talk to, I wasn't able to even formulate the questions in my own mind, let alone put them into words. One way of dealing with this confusion was to internalize it all, bury it away somewhere, and hope that one day an answer would come. But however I "dealt" with it, it had a lasting impact upon my psyche.

I was born in England to parents who were incredibly supportive of my doing what I felt I needed to do. They never told me I could not or should not do anything, but rather they backed me 100% no matter which direction I wandered off in. This was an amazing blessing—even more so in retrospect. So many people are constantly reminded of their place in the world. "You cannot go there, that is not your place." "You cannot do that." "You should do this." "You are a failure." And so on. Sometimes the comments are well meant, sometimes they are said out of a parent's frustration. Sometimes this conditioning—for that is what it is—is obvious. More often it is subtle background noise, but either way, that early indoctrination will stay with that child for life. Whatever the intent or intensity of conditions in our early years, many of us grow up with imposed limitations from which we never manage to completely break free. I have had—and still have—mine.

I recently had two African-American men come to a workshop in San Francisco, a rare event, as plenty of African-American women come to workshops, but no men. Over lunch with one of them, I told him how unusual it was for a person of his background to come to a workshop, and he told me his story. A person of African heritage growing up in the United States,doesn't always have an easy time. He told me he was reminded constantly, by his mother, what he could or could not do, where he could and could not go. From a very early age, he was being told by someone he trusted and loved that he was different, and that difference influenced and limited his future. For whatever reason, he wasn't satisfied with these limitations and set out to discover a different reality. He left his past behind and explored the world, made friends outside of expectations, did things, went places that were closed to others from his background. Because he was not carrying his past with him to such an

obvious degree that many others—from all backgrounds—
do, he did not project that past into his future, and by not
doing that, met with greater equanimity wherever he went.

We had both come from very different backgrounds,
but both ended up in the same place of freedom that
leaving the past behind brings. This freedom that comes
from leaving the past behind is relative to how much we
can let go of and the reality that is our world. For example,
this man was told from an early age what he could expect
to experience in his life, but he chose not to accept those
limitations and set out to discover, for himself, a path of
his own. To some degree, he was successful, but he still
lived and operated in a world that was—to a large extent—
dominated by others, each with their own unique view
of how things were or should be. This man's freedom
of choice was therefore limited to his ability to leave the
past behind and still subject to environmental conditions
outside his control. An important lesson for him, and me,
was to recognize this fact and explore within those society-
based limitations.

To be free of the past is a goal of mine. To be in a place
where the past no longer controls me. I am not there yet.
I still have a way to go, and I recognize how my current
situation has been created by my past. Perhaps we can never
be entirely free from our past. Our past is our heritage, our
history; it is how we place ourselves in the world. It is our
identity, at least it has been in the past. It is how we associate
with and relate to ourselves and others. It is not this past that
I want to be free from, but how our past makes victims of us.
It is how our past conditions us to either respond or react in
predetermined ways that I want to move beyond.

A by-product of part of my history, my heritage, was to make me feel very claustrophobic and limited. Growing up in the United Kingdom, I discovered too many conditions that I sensed were trying to contain me and take me in directions that I felt were not in my best interests. If you have ever suffered from claustrophobia—whether it was a physical issue or whether you felt you were imprisoned inside of yourself—you will understand what I was going through.

There were too many expectations, too much history. At least, that was my perception, and—as I have since discovered—perceptions are everything. Many people are content with their lot, never questioning or traveling far. I often envied them as the restlessness inside me grew and I—still quite young—was not able to understand what or why this was happening to me.

I tried to make my way in England, do what was expected of me, though I am no longer sure who was expecting what—if indeed I ever was. My childhood may or may not have been like the early years of others, I really do not know. I believe that how we perceive what happened to us as children is just as important as what actually happened to us. Two children may experience a very similar upbringing, but each could have a completely different memory of their childhood, as each perceived what was happening in their own unique way.

Our future is in part based upon our perceptions of our past, on the self imposed limitations those perceptions bring with them, and any concept we have of who it is who is actually doing the perceiving.

I never had dreams about what I wanted to do when I "grew up." I had no sense of where I wanted to be years down the path of life. I still don't. Perhaps what was driving me to seek something other than what I was born into, was this feeling of being different, this feeling as though I did not belong. I felt as though someone—or something—had made a very big mistake in causing me to be born when and where I had been. I had a strong feeling of wrong time, wrong place, maybe even wrong planet. When all these feelings started to arise, I was too young to even begin to think that I was questioning the reasons for the human condition here on earth. I just did not feel as though I belonged and wanted to find out why and—if possible—do something about it.

This feeling of difference was not one of superiority, although I was appalled as I watched both personal and global dramas unfolding around me. I simply could not understand man's inhumanity to his fellows, nor his abuse of the planet. I think one of the most important gifts my parents gave me, apart from life itself, was never to say "you cannot do such and such." I grew up having a strong belief in myself and that I could do—or be—anything I chose. At the time, this was not a conscious knowing, but just a state of being, for I had nothing to compare it to.

In spite of my loving parents, I believe I was seriously traumatized in childhood. As tiny children, we see and hear and understand things differently. We often misinterpret a word or a gesture, and our young mind and dependant body has its own way of relating to the big world around us. Our way of interpreting a word or a gesture may be totally different from the intent behind it. If misunderstandings are not picked up quickly and corrected, the memory may well influence us for the rest of our life.

A tendency of the young is to take things out of context and give them far more energy than they deserve. As children, we have the capacity to exaggerate something that we heard or saw out of all proportion. This characteristic is often carried over into adult life, where the conditioning of the past is so strong that a person retains a particular way of dealing with life's situations instead of growing out of it. Being locked into the past like this leads to certain levels of dysfunction in the adult's life, so that the past is simply repeating itself.

Seen from this vantage point, it's possible that I was not traumatized by childhood events at all. Maybe it was all a misunderstanding. Maybe I took something to heart, took something seriously, and have suffered under some misconception ever since.

Age, wisdom, and experience have since brought me to the conclusion that it doesn't really matter what happened or why. What is important for me now is to see how I took what happened to me in the past—whether real or imagined—personally. Through the eyes of the child, I perceived events in a certain way, identified with them, took them seriously, and have consequently been carrying that "conditioning" around with me ever since.

In spite of this identification with my past—or perhaps because of it—I had a well-developed capacity to become totally involved in whatever I was doing. I admit that I was very selective in what I did. I only become involved in things that did not remind me of my (perceived) traumatic past. This is a little survival technique I am sure many of us are expert at. Preferring happiness over discomfort, we are drawn to what gives us pleasure or what we find easy, and we avoid things that confront us or remind us of an unpleasant past.

A side effect of this feeling of claustrophobia was a frustration with tasks that no longer challenged me. It was as though I was a lion in a cage, pacing backward and forward, waiting for an opportunity to escape, waiting for the door to be left open. When that happened, I would be off and running, only to find myself in another cage, engaged in yet another task that I had discovered could distract me from the cause of my agitation. I was back in the cage again, looking for a place of safety and comfort. It took me a few years to discover that I would never find safety and comfort in a cage of busyness.

The moment I had mastered a task I would be off, out of one cage, into another, in an entirely different direction, looking for a new challenge. As the common conception of mastery is that it takes years, possibly lifetimes to become a master, I am not sure I ever actually mastered any task. All I did was reach a place where whatever I was doing no longer held any interest for me. At the time, it manifested in my mind as restlessness. Now I can see that whatever name I used to try and understand what was happening to me, I was simply describing the symptoms. Although I did not recognize it initially, over time, it became clear that I was on a quest, a search for a meaning to my life.

All of this movement—one job to another, one place to another—gives the impression that I simply could not settle down to one thing. And this was absolutely true. The lion needed to be free and could not rest until it was. Some people saw this as a weakness, but those people did not understand me. How could they, when I did not understand myself what was happening or why.

It was not as though I found life in England to be totally oppressive. There were many things for which I am very grateful. But beneath the surface, hidden somewhere deep inside of me was the lion, and that lion wanted out. It had nothing whatsoever to do with living in England. It would not have mattered where I lived. I would have felt the same.

The sense of being contained continued to grow. Perhaps I just resisted it less and less, but the end result was the same. I left England on my journey of self discovery. The lion had, temporarily, escaped his cage. My perception back then was that I would be better able to find myself if I were to leave the past—and with it all that was familiar— behind me. So I set out for Australia, and the "freedom" that anonymity would bring.

Although this was not the first step I had taken, it was a major one. And it is still an ongoing process. It took a few years of being in Australia for me to even begin to work myself free of some of the old conditioning. In the beginning I found I had exchanged one cage for another and realized that I was still looking for the security of the familiar. Yet this cage was different than the cages of the past. This one was in a country where no one knew me or my past—and better still—no one cared what my past had been.

This new place gave me more freedom, and this—in turn—allowed me to become more aware of the person inside, still trying to get out. I became more aware of the old conditioning, so that—even though I was not yet free of the past—I was able to become more aware of how it had shaped—and was continuing to shape—my life. For many of us, our lives remain a product of that early conditioning, and we rarely question it because it is such an integral part of who we think we are.

Deep down inside me there was still something wanting to be discovered and this something kept pushing me along a path that I did not even know I was on. Sometimes I would wander off the path—or so it seemed—but mostly I took every opportunity to travel, to explore, to seek answers. It appeared that I was a nomad at heart, a wanderer in search of whatever answers life has to offer. I traveled extensively throughout Australia, I spent many years in Southeast Asia, sailing, exploring, just being with the local people—all in a never-ending quest for my personal holy grail.

But I had gotten lost looking for answers externally. For years, I traveled, sometimes losing myself in the journey, getting sidetracked, as I spent time taking myself way too seriously. Sooner or later though, every side road would exhaust itself, and I would be back where I started, still trying to make sense of my life. This external seeking went on for many years, but over time, it became a journey into the self, one where I no longer sought answers outside of myself.

I had had an intuitive understanding of the teachings of the Buddha from a very early age, although I had no idea where this knowing came from. It certainly wasn't a backlash from a Christian religious upbringing, as my parents were not particularly religious. It was not a rebellion, it was just there, and I am still not sure why it was or where it came from. Back in childhood, I could no more understand what was happening to me than I could understand the physics of putting people into space. It is very difficult for us to question who we are. It is so much easier to question the actions and values of others.

I spent many hours with the monks in Sri Lanka, conversing with them with ease, often on deep, complicated subjects. I still wondered where this "knowing" of mine came from. I never did get any satisfactory answers and finally just accepted that I knew things that many people around me either weren't interested in or had never even heard of. As a result of my travels to Sri Lanka and Thailand, my journey began to take on a more overt sense of a spiritual quest. Of course, it had never been anything other than that, but I was too young and naive to know what was really happening.

I had not done—and still have not done—much formal study on the teachings of the Buddha. I have not done much formal study on any spiritual teachings. It is not who I am—at least at the moment. But to the best of my ability, I have tried to live the teachings of the Buddha and to share my understanding of the Dharma as a foundation to my life. Looking back, I can see how limited my understanding was and am grateful for those I shared with for their understanding—or lack of it—and for the kindness they offered. I know that I will look back on this time of my life in the future and think how naive and limited my understanding was, and how the people I shared with were kind enough not to laugh out loud at me.

Life is an amazing thing with its miracle of reproduction and the incredible diversity of life's many manifestations. For the purpose of this book, the most important thing of all is in the way we relate to life itself, the way we understand it, the way we learn to be with it. How we contribute to the miracle. What we choose and what we do with our time here.

What amazes me the most though is that we don't seem to have changed much over the millennia. We still make the same decisions, we still suffer the same conflicts, we play the same parts, and act out the same dramas in the same way that we have done for a very long time indeed. Nothing really changes.

We may hope for different times, for more peace, more harmony, but, as Albert Einstein said, we cannot successfully fix a "problem" from the same level of awareness that created it. When we habitually do we wonder why we still get more of the same. Once we realize that the same old roles from the past are again being recreated—only by different actors this time—we start to see how the reality that has manifested on this planet has been playing by the same rules for a long, long time. There really is nothing for us to do if we are content with more of the same in our future.

We seem to have conditioned ourselves to believe that the only way to solve a problem is to either legislate against it, feed it, stop feeding it, pour money into it, shoot it, or ignore it. If any of these methods had worked in the past, surely we have been doing it long enough now that there should be no problems left. Why do we continue to try and solve the problems of the world through these outdated—and obviously ineffectual—methods? Perhaps when we understand why we do this, we will see a new way and start applying it.

The old ways of solving problems do not work. They have never worked, and they will never work. This is witnessed by the fact that modern society is facing the same issues that societies have faced in the past. Feeding the starving is good, educating those without education is good, clothing and housing those who have lost everything is good. It is good when those who have money provide support to those who do not. Yet, without a new way of seeing and working with what is creating the imbalance in the first place, any good deeds are ultimately doomed to failure. If we continue to approach the problem from the same old place, our solution never really deals with it, and the problem, as such, never goes away. It will just require more food, more money, more clothes, more control. In fact, a never-ending supply of energy, in its many forms, would be necessary to just even scratch the surface of the problems the world faces.

People with any social conscience come from the best of intentions when they seek change. It is a part of human nature to want to help those less fortunate than oneself. Yet without making changes on a fundamental level, those people are going to be busy for a very long time. They will always be trying to stop the leaks, to prevent the boat from sinking, instead of realizing where the real problems lie. As we patch one leak, another appears, and so it goes. Perhaps there are people who do see through all the layers to the root cause of the suffering of others. Without understanding this cause of suffering people may feel powerless to make any changes required. Perhaps the task is just too big for them, and they merely resign themselves to doing the best they can. Indeed, is there any other way to change the way of the world?

I used to feel hurt and get very angry at all the injustice in the world, with all its violence and abuse. I could not watch the news on television without getting upset, so eventually I just had to stop watching TV. What could I do to change anything? I had no skills that were in demand, I had very little money, I just did not know where to start. I was witnessing so many acts of abuse in so many areas that it was hard to pick one as being more valid than any other. Going with my heart did not help either—I was torn in too many directions with the result that I was left feeling pretty useless.

I was seeing people working to save this and that, always making a difference, but next week, there they were again, back at it. Everyone seemed to be battling with the same monster—the monster of greed, fear, and ignorance. No matter how much you influenced the multitude of manifestations of the monster, turn around, and there was something else that needed your time and energy. Like the Hydra, the many headed monster—chop one off and two more grew. How could I possibly make a difference?

It's not that I think it is pointless to fight the monster, but I think our time might be better spent seeing what creates the monster and work at dismantling it on that level.

It is not capitalism, it is not communism, nor any other "ism." They are all manifestations of the monster. The problem—and the answer to it—I believe, can be found in each and every person's heart.

So, once I had spent some time feeling useless, I realized that I, personally, could do nothing, given who I felt myself to be at the time. More importantly, I came to the realization that for me to have any "positive" impact upon the world, I had first to change myself.

I recognized that every time I supported any issue, I became a part of the problem. There was always an "us"

and a "them." So if there is an us and a them, there is a
good and a bad, and, of course, I was always on the side of
the good! I saw that by my associating with either side of
the cause, I actually supported the conflict by adding fuel
to the fire, even though I was on the side of right! I was still
a part of the problem. Of course, the people on the other
side of the fence also believed they were in the right. They
had their own reasons, which they were able to justify, as I
was able to justify mine. There were two groups of people,
each thinking they were right, defending their position
against a threat to their values, perhaps even thinking god
is on their side.

The group with the most money, or access to money,
more lawyers, or more power often wins the argument.
If the two sides are equally matched, then there will be a
compromise. This is how we resolve differences in the 21st
century, and the way we resolved differences of opinion in
the Dark Ages was no different, though I doubt there were
as many lawyers around then. Short of major catastrophes—
or enlightenment—we will be resolving our differences the
same way in the year 3,000. Not a very comforting thought.

It seems to me that we are trying to resolve differences
that should never have arisen in the first place, differences
that are only a reflection of a much greater turmoil that
is taking place. It is failing to understand the process that
creates this external conflict, this us and them mentality.

Exercise

Reflect for a moment on the evolution, the history of
mankind. Where have we come from, and where are we

going? Have you ever really questioned where you come from? Do you believe what has been written? Is faith in another's belief enough?

Try and imagine, how problems were dealt with in the past, and see if you can notice any difference in how those same problems are dealt with today. Are the problems still the same? Do we still have the same way of dealing with them? Has our problem solving ability evolved? Or not?

Chapter Two
We and the Spaces We Live in

I am sure that many of us are aware that unseen energies in our environment are affecting us every moment of our lives. Some of these energies are common knowledge, such as, X-rays, gamma rays, the radiation from the sun. These energies are a natural part of the world we live in, and whilst systems remain in a balanced state—both your's and the earth's—these energies will not have a negative impact upon you. We are seeing certain frequencies of sunlight in various parts of the world being blamed for higher rates of skin cancers, and this, to me, is an indication of a system out of balance, at least a balance that humans find comfortable. Being the dominant species on the planet, we assume the role of yardstick and measure balance as a world we can comfortably survive in.

In recent years, we have been exposed to more extremely low electromagnetic frequencies than ever before. Many lives have been changed dramatically by the readily available electricity that now powers our homes, our offices, and industries. Anyone with a device designed to measure magnetic and electrical fields can demonstrate that the energy from power stations, power lines, and even appliances is not contained within them. Both the electrical and magnetic components of the electrical supply can be measured as impacting the environment at some distance from the power lines or the appliances themselves.

There are ongoing discussions, backed up by numerous studies, about the effects this radiation has upon the human body. It is not my intention to take sides in this argument. I long ago stopped taking too much notice of all the studies. For me, it was impossible to sort out fact from fiction. The language used in such reports was beyond my ability to interpret it, There were plenty of "facts" and figures, which ultimately supported one point of view over another, but they rarely made any sense to me. I have seen reports that support both sides of the argument, and, from those reports, I really cannot tell who is right and who is wrong.

I believe they are both right, and they are both wrong. When people set out to find something, they generally succeed. They discover "facts" that support their belief. No doubt, there are exceptions, where people arrive at a destination they never expected or knew to be there, but this is not what I am referring to here. It is the science that sets out to validate a presumption or expectation that I question.

There are multiple reasons why people elect to believe in one report over another, and rarely can you get anyone to change their minds. It is a very sacred and emotive area, the world of our personal beliefs.

Now, significant increases in the levels and frequencies of man-made microwave radiation has been added to this cosmic soup mix in which we all live. There is no doubt our environment has undergone major changes in the last 100 years.

When I was introduced to these and other frequencies that could impact the health or well-being of large numbers of people I knew that this was an important step on my journey. At the time, I did not understand the full significance of this realization, just that it was important and profound. Realizing just how significant an impact the space we live in could have upon our well-being opened my eyes to a very different reality. This step would eventually to lead me into working with people and the land and, ultimately, teaching.

Later, when I discovered how simple it was to restore balance to the energy in a home or workplace, I began to see how I could use this understanding to help me move out of my old limitations by applying it and combining it with my own background.

My introduction to the world of space clearing has been dealt with in detail in my book, *The Moment That Matters*, but, for those of you not familiar with it, I will explain briefly here.

Many years ago while living in South Australia, I was introduced to a man who was giving workshops on clearing the energy of space. Essentially this looked at how certain environmental energies were affecting people's health, wealth, and happiness. I saw something in this work that appealed very strongly to me and took the workshop.

The theory was fascinating—how unseen energies of the earth, electrical fields, and even events that had occurred in the environment could all affect those who lived within the range of such energies. I found the application of devices to change the energy more challenging. Although the methods we used to restore balance to the environment seemed to work, and the feedback from clients was very positive, I was not happy using them. I did not like the role of judge, nor was I convinced that in restoring balance I truly knew what I was doing. People would see me as some sort of Mr. Fix-it, which did not sit well with me. I was beginning to see how it was not only the energy of space that was out of balance. It was the relationship of the people in the space to the energies that was a big part of the problem they were experiencing.

In the early days of my consulting on clearing the energy of space, it quickly became apparent to me that simply by showing up, I was affecting the space, often in a more positive way than I found it. It took a long time for me to even begin to understand and integrate this, but as I did, I moved away from using any formula, object, or device to bring balance back into homes and businesses.

I also saw how some people I worked for could not hold the change but how the energy of the space would return to old patterns within weeks of the consults. This could either be through some fault of mine or because of the part the clients played in co-creating their own space. More research indicated this was indeed the problem. Some people keep seeking without accepting any responsibility, so no matter who they called in, nothing seemed to hold.

Once I began working with environmental energies in people's homes and workplaces, I often noticed a direct relationship between the energy of the home and that of the people living there. It often seemed to me that the energy in the home was, in part, a product of the energy of those living in the space. This was not always the case, as many times the people in the house seemed to be victims to energies that were beyond their control. But increasingly, I noticed how the mental or emotional state of the people living in the house was reflected in the various energy fields I was working with. It was as though the physical, emotional, and mental energy of the people living in the home was affecting the energy of the space around them. This is pretty much common knowledge to me now, but when I first understood the reciprocal relationship between how we impact our space and how our space impacts us, it was a very exciting breakthrough.

If you are feeling low, imagine how the energy of your space can take on and reflect that feeling back to you. And because the space seemingly supports your low feeling, how hard it would be to find your way out of it when you are surrounded by it all the time.

How often have we picked up on a feeling when stepping into someone else's home—a light feeling or maybe a dark, heavy, or happy one. These are all words we use to describe how we feel in a space, and how the space makes us feel. Many factors have to be taken into account when we try to work out what makes us feel a certain way in any particular environment—not least the people who actually live in that space. Sometimes the energy of the space is enough to make someone living in that space uncomfortable. The challenge is knowing when it is you and when it is the space.

In all of the consultations I did, it became increasingly obvious to me that the people who lived in the space could be a major part of any problem. It was not always the energy of the space that was the real problem people were encountering in their homes. The real issue was often the relationship the people had both with the energy in their homes and with themselves. Out of this understanding, I developed the personal clearing that I used in association with the space clearing.

It was a powerful time for me, seeing how each of us contributes to the world around us simply by being in that world. Our personal world becomes a reflection of who we are. We all affect our environment consciously by what we do and say, but we contribute so much more without any awareness whatsoever that we are doing it.

As long as we remain unaware of the energetic effect we are having on our environment, little can be done to change it. There are many different approaches to restoring greater balance and harmony in a home, and all may have varying degrees of success. Yet, if the inhabitants themselves are responsible for the imbalance, until they change, there can be no lasting improvement in the energy of the home.

As this deeper understanding of our relationship with our environment grew in me, I started to see that many of the reasons people called me in for a consultation could be traced back to their own attitude or perceptions. I became aware that many of the problems people perceived they were experiencing were more about their relationship to themselves, to others, and to the external world than about the space itself.

I had not set out to prove this, in fact, I was not even aware that this way of relating was even a possibility before I began to study this. That I did not have to prove to myself that this was so made it easier. I have quite an open mind, and this allows me to take new information, play with it for a while, accept what I can and leave what I cannot. It means that I do not reject information simply because it is new to me, or because it is not commonly accepted as "real."

So I played with this new way of looking at life for a long time, not with a naive acceptance, but with an inquiring mind. I was reminded of the words, reportedly spoken by Jesus the Christ, "except as little children shall ye come to me ..." The innocence, the openness, the willingness to explore and accept may well be the simple key to everlasting life. Adults tend to get bogged down in routine—routine ways of doing things, routine ways of seeing things, routine ways of reacting to situations. I have, to the best of my ability, avoided that path as much as possible, preferring to be as open as I can and to explore what comes my way, instead of rejecting it out of hand.

Before I started studying this subject, I had no idea that people's immediate environment could have such an impact on their health. But as time went on, I found that a common reason for people to call me in for a consult was health issues. One or more people in the house may have been sick, and no matter what they did, they could not seem to shake the problem. They may have heard about me from a friend, and, out of desperation or frustration, called me in to see if there was anything happening in the house energetically that was either causing or contributing to their state of ill health. I was often able to locate and identify various energies in the space that could well be contributing to the poor health people were experiencing. This was demonstrated to be true when, having brought balance back to their environment, all signs of sickness went away.

But it was not always the case that it was the environment that was making the people sick or depressed. Even when I was able to detect energies in the space that could be having a detrimental affect on the inhabitants, I could never be sure what had come first. Were the disturbing energies already in the house, and the people inherited them when they moved in? Or did they bring the disturbances with them? Were the inhabitants directly responsible for the imbalance in the energy of their home?

These are not always easy questions to answer. The relationship we have with our environment is so much a part of who we are that it is sometimes difficult to know where one finishes and the other begins. Even if I located energy that I assumed was causing or contributing to the inhabitants' health issues, it still came down to the perceptions, conscious or not of the people living in the house. It was the relationship of the person to both internal and external energy that was the key to change.

Most people had not noticed the connection for themselves, just as I had not noticed it before I began to study this phenomenon. They had not even considered how what they were feeling could have been either stimulated or caused by energies in their environment or that their feelings were influencing those energies. It is just not something most people think about. Lack of awareness, however, does not mean we are not affected. It just means we do not know the reason why we feel whatever it is we are feeling. We are adding to, changing, and influencing our environment constantly, and we do all this mostly without awareness, subconsciously, simply by being who we are. And we, in turn, are being changed and influenced by that environment every moment of the day, usually in very subtle ways that can and do accumulate over time.

I had already realized that in order to change our world we first needed to change ourselves. And this realization taught me how much of an impact each of us has on the space we inhabit, and how—literally, by changing our mind—we can change the energy of the space.

This concept may not be quite that easy to grasp for someone caught up in the limitations of the personality, but with a little guidance and a willingness to have an open mind, it becomes obvious and simple. It is so simple that many people find it difficult to comprehend, for we are brought up in a world that values complexity, values the act of doing, a world that believes the more complex the doing, the more powerful the result.

The key to change was now so obvious I could not doubt it. And now, I had seen ways that I could employ on the journey, ways that I could share with others, ways that were more tangible than words or concepts

This changing the self, however, has been much harder than I thought it would be. In fact, had I known beforehand how hard it would be, I might never have started on the journey.

No, that is not true. I could no more have stopped myself than I could have stopped breathing. I could not even have had second thoughts, for, although we may be warned of dangers on the road ahead, we still need to find out for ourselves what those dangers are. We face them and move beyond—or not—but this is the life we must lead. In the workshops I try and help people become aware of some of the challenges they may face; they smile and nod, and then forget I ever said anything of the sort and proceed to learn through their own experiences. This is good, this is how it must be, for we cannot learn by the experiences of others, we cannot accept on faith the lessons to be learned but must find out for ourselves.

But the journey to change the self, this is the wonderful part. As you talk the talk and walk the walk, you discover so much about yourself, your relationship with others, and the world around you that not only can you never be the same person who started on this journey, you don't want to be. As you discover how incredibly powerful you are, how you understand—possibly for the first time—how your thoughts, words, and deeds do truly add to and influence the world around you, your life will change forever. Then you may see that there could be other ways to solve your problems and the problems of the world—the way of the fearless heart, sometimes called the immaculate heart. This is a place of understanding and sharing, a path that is both so simple and powerful you cannot understand why you never tried it before.

This book is about my ongoing journey and that of many others like me who have discovered or are discovering the power of the compassionate heart. People are quietly applying this way of being to every moment and every situation in their lives and are finding the huge and amazing difference it makes—not just to their own lives, but to the lives of family and friends and to their personal and global environments.

To better understand how and why we are who we are, it would help us to get a different point of view on our origins—where we came from, why and how that perception is maintained.

Here I remind you not to believe a word I say. This is just a story—my story.

Exercise

Have you noticed how, in some places you feel good, and other places not so good? Do you know why this is? Is it the people in your environment? Or is it the environment itself?

Can you tell the difference? What is it about other people or the environment that can affect how you feel?

Practice noticing how your feelings change when the people around you change, at home; at work; in your social life.

Why do some people feel great in a forest and others great in a city?

Chapter Three
Why We Are Who We Are

We accept, for the most part, that we are our personality. It is something we are born with, something that evolves as a result of our social conditioning and of our personal experiences. We do not question the validity of this personality. Yet if we do ever question who we are, the questions asked will be limited to the awareness of the personality asking the questions. It would seem that it cannot be any other way.

How can we even begin to contemplate questions that are outside of our being, outside of our range of experience, outside of our current worldview? No matter how broad-minded we consider ourselves to be, we can still only ask questions that are formulated from within the personality.

To give you an example, before my introduction to working with the energies of the environment, it would never have entered my mind to question my relationship to my environment. The package of who I was at the time, ergo my personality, could not ask the question because it was not aware. As it evolved, in part because of an open, questioning mind, it became aware and asked the question.

Yet to understand the nature of the personality, how it is formed, where it comes from, and how it is sustained is the first step to freedom from the limitations imposed by our identification with that very personality. Yet here we may be caught in a Catch-22 situation. What limitations are we referring to? And why do we need to be free of them? Until we realize how our life is controlled by our association with our personality, there can be no desire to be free from those limitations. Until we take the first step toward this realization, there is no apparent need to take any steps at all.

We associate strongly with likes and dislikes, thoughts and feelings, ideas, goals, judgments, memories, and experiences. All of these things, these parts, these thoughts, beliefs and feelings make up the personality we believe ourselves to be. There is the body of course, the temple, the vehicle that houses the personality that we also mistake for who we are.

Most of us identify so totally with the physical body that to think—even for a moment—that this isn't who we really are seems ridiculous. Yet, if we want to question this age-old perception, that we are the body, that we are the personality, we must have a starting point, a frame of reference. We need a safe place so that once we begin to see that all is not as it appears, we have some safe ground we can retreat to, a familiar place to take stock.

As long as we so strongly associate with the body and personality as being who we are, then the problems of the world—if indeed there are any problems with the world— will be reduced to concepts and images that the personality can deal with. Having reduced the issues to something manageable, we attempt to fix the problems from within the understanding and abilities of our personality.

Therein, to my mind, lies the real problem. We are trying to fix something, that may or may not be broken, based on our perceptions of good and bad, right and wrong, and we impose our will to correct the problem. Our will, being personality-based, is hardly in any position to evaluate what is best for another; it can barely take care of itself. If we, personally, have not climbed above the tree line of limiting human perceptions, then it is unrealistic to expect ourselves to be able to see a bigger picture beyond the forest. And if we cannot see the bigger picture, how can we expect to help others see that picture?

Yet it is very much a part of human nature to try and fix the problems of others whilst ignoring our own personal issues. Externalize the problem, and you won't have to look at yourself. It's so much easier to try to correct the imbalances in the lives of others than in our own life.

But who or what is this personality? Where did it come from? What created it?

It is commonly accepted that our physical forms are the product of the coming together of the sperm and the egg, a miracle in itself. A baby human is conceived, and, invariably is born into the world. It is also widely held that while the physical characteristics of the human baby are a result of the genetics of the parents, each baby is physically, emotionally, and mentally unique. What makes each baby unique is a combination of many factors— parents' genetics, parents' emotional and mental state at the time of conception and during the pregnancy, and many others. To my mind, the genetic memory only goes so far in explaining who we think we are. There are many other aspects that are not so readily accepted, for example, the possibility of a soul memory that I will introduce later as a means to try and explain the uniqueness of individuals from another perspective.

My brother, my sister, and I all came from the same gene pool, our mother and father, but we are each as different as chalk and cheese, physically, mentally, and emotionally. If it was purely and simply a matter of genes, one would expect that we would be more alike. Perhaps soul memory will help account for the marked differences.

If we look just at the genetics for the moment and see that our physical body is a product of our parents' genetic memory, then it should follow that our parents' bodies are products of their parents' genetic memories. And so it goes, each physical generation a product of the genetic history of its past.

We can explore later on how memory, genetic or soul, can get passed down from generation to generation and the impact this has upon the baby. It should be clear though that, to a large extent, we are the product of our parents' experiences and they, in turn, were products of their parents' experiences. This was, until recently, the popular belief, and no doubt still is in many circles.

If genetic history were the only factor to take into consideration, it should still be clear that we are a product of the past, and we can be nothing else. But it isn't. As Dr. Bruce Lipton, Ph.D tells us, there is more to who we are than pre-programmed genetic memory: "It is now recognized that the environment, and more specifically, our perception (interpretation) of the environment, directly controls the activity of our genes.

Recognizing that our genes can be affected by our environment opens the doors to some very interesting perceptions. Not the least of which is a confirmation of my findings in the relationship between people and their environments, and how we are affected by so called "external" phenomena.

Yet there is still room for genetic history to help us understand who we are, where we came from, and possibly, where we are going.

During some of my travels, I recognized that I was experiencing some of these adventures on behalf of my father. I was doing things he had wanted to do, but because of circumstances, had not been able to do. He was living through me. This realization did not trouble me. It wasn't as though I could separate myself from the life I was living even had I wanted to. I had no resistance to the traveling and the lifestyle—it was, after all, who I felt myself to be. Indeed it was a very important part of my search for self; it just happened to be an unlived aspect of my fathers' life as well.

I have come to understand that had I not lived this for my father, I could have passed this memory on to my son, and then he would have had to decide whether to live that life or not. I chose to live that life. It suited me and the journey I had undertaken, and the fact that I was able to help my father was a big bonus. I was aware that this small part of my life was not totally my own but a combination of desires—mine and my father's. How much more was I not aware of? How many other aspects of the life I live are still other people, my ancestors, living life through me? I have a sense that there was, or is, a lot more of my parents living through me than I am aware of, but I can never be sure.

It is interesting how the idea that our environment is affecting our genes opens up and gives strength to the mind-body connection, the part that our perceptions of self play in creating our worldview. Even had I not been affected to the degree I thought I was by my mother and father's genetic contributions to my life and its subsequent self perception, I was still affected by their thoughts and feelings. They were as much my inheritance as their genes.

But it is food for thought to ask, how much of any life is living out or completing aspects of its genetic, mental, or emotional past? Most of us just pass our memories on to our children without any awareness whatsoever. There is often the idea that your children will keep the family line going, which is obviously true. But to what degree is what you give your children a reflection of who you are, and what does it mean? We identify with and are so lost in our personal drama, this part we are playing, that it is very difficult to step out of the part or the drama and see ourselves objectively. This is not a criticism, it is not good or bad, but merely human nature to be so involved in the drama.

Back to the unborn baby, created from the parents. If my understanding was correct, that I had indeed lived some of "my" life for my parents, then that was being programmed into the little baby that was me as it developed prior to birth. Part of me thinks, "how can it be otherwise," but there are many levels, many other possibilities yet to explore.

The more we explore our origins and what makes us who we perceive ourselves to be, the more we are exposed to the concept of the mind-body connection. The more we understand the nature of mind, the greater difficulty we have in pinning the mind down to any time and place. There is nothing new about the concept of non-local mind, how the mind is not confined to time and space, but what interests me is what we can do with this information, and where it will take us. It certainly adds a new dimension to genetics, which we shall look at from different angles in the following chapters.

When the baby is born it brings with it certain information that has been passed on from the parents through genes or possibly some other, non-physical, connection. This inheritance will influence the development of the child in many ways, for example, by helping to create certain likes and dislikes, establish the beginnings of a pre-programmed set of values and judgments, and certain attitudes and aptitudes. It is the foundation for the unique personality that you are and will be.

You were born with the programming that included your physical attributes. You were born into a particular era, in a particular country. You had a language that you grew to identify with. You may have had a particular ethnic group that you associated with, and you would certainly have had a social group, a financial group, maybe a political group, and possibly some religious affiliation as well. All of these— passed on by your parents and your immediate society— have helped shape who you perceive yourself to be today.

So now you have a vehicle, a body in which to experience life for yourself. This body comes with its ancestral memories, its genetic conditioning based on the past and, over time, its developed associations with its social and environmental conditions.

To help visualize how certain memories—which may hold unresolved issues, ancestral or otherwise—can influence us, I often refer to those sort of memories as having a charge. This "charge" is similar to the charge held by a battery—positive or negative, but not in the sense of being good or bad. It is just information that is stored and has yet to find release or balance. However, using the word "charge" will help us understand how we can be the victim of unresolved memories—the bigger the charge, the stronger, more intense our association with the memory, and the more likely we are to be a victim to that information without necessarily being aware that this is happening.

I believe it is likely that you come in to this life with soul memory—for want of a better description—which may have its own charge and which will influence your likes, your dislikes, and your decisions. This concept of soul memory can be a sticky one. Some people accept it easily, with or without questioning its validity, while some people's beliefs do not allow them to even consider the idea of a soul memory. I will use it, as I mentioned above, for want of a better description, to try and explain certain phenomena that may be otherwise unexplainable.

The young baby is going to be affected by its environment and by those in that environment, parents, siblings, other relatives, family friends, and these people will—with or without awareness—shape the life of the infant for years to come. Remember, we are looking at the coming together of two "packets" of information here, the genetic memory of the child's parents and ancestors, and the child's own soul memory.

Our genetic history gives us the physical body and all of its attributes, including some mental and emotional memory. The soul memory may well give us a sense of purpose and other aspects that are not so easily explained by genetics. For example, where did my intuitive knowing of the words of the

Buddha come from? There are several possibilities that I am aware of, and possibly more that I am not aware of.

Here we need to diverge for a moment to get a better understanding of these possibilities.

I realize that many people reading this will have little difficulty in accepting the concept of a soul memory, yet there may be some who question this idea. I consider myself to have always been quite an open-minded person who did not shut out information merely because it may have sounded way out or ridiculous. I did not simply accept everything I was told, but I was open—on neutral ground as it were—not dismissing information just because it was not currently in vogue.

Simply because ideas are not held by the majority doesn't mean those ideas are not valid. I have always wanted to decide on the validity of beliefs, concepts, and ideas, for myself, as they may apply to me. It was important to me not to be swayed by the collective into believing what everyone else believed, nor to exclude information that was not accepted by the collective.

I may be what some would call a free-thinker, and this has helped me sort through ideas and concepts, evaluate them by exploring, questioning, and applying them, and then either accepting or letting go. It is never simple, never just black or just white, and I may take a little of this, a little of that. If it made sense at the time and was valuable, if it added to my knowledge and wisdom, then great. I also recognize that as we understand more, or perhaps more precisely, as we change and grow, ideas and concepts that once served us fall away to be replaced by other ideas and concepts. We cannot hold onto the past, for the only constant

I have discovered on this journey into self, is change. So many personal and global problems arise through a lack of understanding of this concept of change with people trying to force change on themselves or others or people trying to resist change.

By trying to be open, I can allow for the possibility of a very different reality to the one most people experience. By doing my best to be conscious about being open, I am aware—to varying degrees—how I do or do not hold judgment around the realities that present themselves. It is difficult for me to be totally objective about the realities that present because the bigger picture is not apparent. I do what I can with what I have at any given moment.

It's not that I accept all so-called "weird stuff" just because it is out there. Much of it I listen to, file away, and if there is ever occasion to recall and use that information, I will, but otherwise it just lies dormant. It is true that I don't take a lot of the stories I am told very seriously, as stories told by an ego-dominated personality may be interesting, but they likely have little real value or truth in them. Because it is so difficult for a person lost in identification with a personality to be objective, their explanations of any issue they experience will always be very subjective reports.

To the best of my ability—given that I, too, am lost in the drama of the personality—I discriminate and try and be as objective as possible, to sort through information, select what seems valid to me or what will help me move on, and discard the rest. As I said a earlier though, we do change, and what was valid once may have served its purpose and needs to be let go to allow for something new, something different, to come in and take its place.

If you break your leg, a crutch will help you get around until the bone heals and you can walk unaided again, you don't carry the crutch around with you just in case you break your leg again. So it is with concepts, with information. Use it, apply it but don't get hung up on it because truth is relative.

This background is just to help explain why I allow for the possibility of soul memory because it is useful at this point in time and will suffice until I come to a greater realization. I did not simply accept soul memory without questioning. I still do question the validity, or likelihood, of this being true. There are other possible ways of explaining things that we are aware of, knowledge that we have without consciously acquiring it, skills that seem to be an integral part of us that genetics cannot explain.

If we can truly develop the ability to question everything around us, everything we are told, everything we read, we might just find that very little of it holds any real truth for us. If people—scientists included—ask questions, they do so from within the framework of the personality and will mostly only find what they are looking for. We may set out to look for the truth, whatever that may be for us at that time, but the answer to any question has to fit our current worldview, or it will not even register on the radar screen. As we expand our worldview, so we are able to receive more information—still not necessarily the truth—but perhaps a little closer to the truth than previously.

So, soul memory.

How can we explain a very young child playing the piano brilliantly, where there is no record of music in the genetic history? How can we explain certain desires and skills that have not shown up in the family's past? How can we explain my intuitive knowing of the teachings of the Buddha. How can we explain the difference between me and my siblings? My brother seems to have been born in the wrong country 150 years too late, as he has an intuitive knowing of the life of a cowboy in the United States. Where did that come from?

Perhaps we have all been hard-wired, if that is possible, to access certain information or skills. If we go down that path, remaining open and questioning, then we are going to have to ask, at some point along the way: if we have been hard wired, then who did it? How? And why?

God is too easy an answer, as it is accepting a concept on faith. Even if we did accept the idea that god did the hard-wiring, it doesn't answer the question of why ... Why do I understand the teachings of the Buddha, and my brother understands the old West? If the hard wiring idea is correct, then it begets another question—hard-wired into what?

I have some ideas on that, but it is going to take some explaining.

Even the concept of soul memory requires that a) we believe in the idea that there is a soul and b) that soul has had other experiences, the memory of which it carries over into other experiences. This then implies that we have had "other" lives, and we get into the area of reincarnation, a whole new ball game around which people have strong views.

I currently choose to believe that there is a soul, that this soul is not limited to this physical body and that the soul may have memory. It explains a lot, and until a better explanation comes along, it will do.

I do have difficulty in accepting the idea of "past lives. Yet, without a comprehensive understanding of our true nature I find it hard to argue for or against this idea. If there is such a thing as "past lives" then it would help explain certain phenomena that I have experienced. Without accepting the soul what is there to carry over from one life to another?

This whole idea is fascinating to me; the exploration of human consciousness is indeed the final frontier. Inner space holds the answers, not outer space.

The body is born, spends a few years on this planet, then dies. If you are your body, then it's curtains for you. If you also believe you are your personality, the concepts you received via the genetic memory of your ancestors, the body, as the vehicle that gives the personality the opportunity to have the experience on planet Earth, is still going to die one day. What happens to who you thought you were?

You may have children, and they will carry the genetics, and perhaps have children of their own, but what happened to you? If you have seriously questioned your existence in this physical body, there must have been moments when you wondered, who the heck am I? Seriously questioning does not mean taking the words or teachings of another on faith and settling back into some personal dreamtime. Serious questioning discards all information previously accepted as the truth, for truth is always relative. Questioning opens the door to allow other information in, without accepting everything that arises in your awareness; you just allow for other possibilities.

Call it what you will, but as we need some language to help us get by, we can settle on soul memory for the time being. The ideas of both soul memory and the hard-wiring may make more—or less—sense as we work our way through to a greater understanding of who we are, where we came from and, possibly, where we are going.

It would appear that we are created in the physical form of the baby with charge or information from our ancestors. Where those ancestors have unfinished business, it may have been passed down through genetics to you. That charge or information passed down may include disease and the state of our emotional and mental health. If your ancestors held a particular belief pattern over a period of time, which was self-limiting or self-destructive, that may have gotten locked into genetic memory. Add to that soul memory, and it becomes increasingly difficult to work out what is yours. And let us not forget that your perceptions may be influencing your genes, reinforcing or reducing ancestral memories. It is one of the intentions of this work to demonstrate that much of who you think you are has nothing to do with you at all. It is only who you think you are. Those perceptions again.

Exercise

Why are we who we are?

Can your earthly experiences account for all that you know, all that you are? Can you see how your genetic history has created who you believe yourself to be?

Are you different from other members of your immediate family? Can you explain this difference?

Without doing this is a judgmental way, compare yourself to your mother, your father, siblings. For some, they are all peas from the same pod, for others, there are significant differences.

Without giving ot a lot of time or energy, just notice, what your differences are. If you do find differences, how would you explain them?

Chapter Four
Reaction or Response?

We have briefly explored the different avenues through which information gathers and enters into the body to create the form and personality that is you. Now we can take a look at how that information can be reinforced.

What seems to be a perfectly natural part of the human condition is to associate and identify with thoughts and feelings that arise in the consciousness/body of the individual. When a thought arises in your awareness, you think that it is your thought because it is happening to you. You are conditioned to believe it must be yours. When an emotion arises in your awareness, you think it is yours as well. Because it's happening in your heart, inside your body, it must be yours. Who else could it possibly belong to? I am feeling this, I am feeling that. I feel glad, I feel sad, I feel sick, I feel tired. Therefore, this is my feeling. I am thinking this, I am thinking that, therefore, this is my thought.

There is an old saying "As you think, so you become." Recent discoveries in science and medicine seem to be confirming it.

In her book, *Biology of Emotion*, Dr. Candace Pert, Ph.D. presents a very different way of looking at who we are and how we get that way. She reports that when we have a thought or a feeling, there is an associated electrical stimulation in the brain. This electrical storm creates a chemical reaction in the body which, in turn, produces neuro-peptides and amino acids. So the body actually produces chemicals associated with certain thoughts and feelings. The more we associate with these thoughts or feelings, the more chemicals the body produces. Mine is an very simplistic explanation of what is really going on, but it does set the scene upon which we can build a very new picture of what is happening inside of us 24 hours a day.

We are conditioned by our past, and because of the nature of that past, we continue to reinforce those old patterns, even handing them down to our children. We may have thought that a newborn baby has no past, but we have to remember to take into account the genetics and the soul memory. To a large degree, this past dictates how we will react to certain information that presents or arises in our awareness. The body of the baby and its associated personality is really the foundation out of which all subsequent experiences arises. How the child deals with life's events will shape how the child will develop, and what happens to the child will influence that child's later life in often profound ways.

When the child repeatedly identifies with the thoughts and feelings that arise in its awareness, neural pathways, connections in the neural net of the brain, are developed. A particular thought creates a particular neural connection, and each neural connection releases certain chemicals associated with that connection, thought, or feeling into the body.

Now the old saying, "As we think, so we become" is demonstrated in the chemistry of the body. If I were to feel nauseous, I might put the feeling down to something I ate. This is the old, traditional way of dealing with a thought or a feeling but, even though this may be the case, it is not necessarily the best way, as we shall see.

Our research through countless workshops has demonstrated that the feeling of nausea may have nothing to do with what you ate, it may instead have been triggered by external phenomena, earth energies, electro-magnetic radiation, emotional energy of others. As long as we maintain the attitude that we are separate, isolated individuals, not connected in any way to our external environment, it is difficult to even begin to accept that we can be influenced by this environment.

There is an exercise in the workshops to demonstrate the relationship we have with the energy of the earth, electrical fields, and other energies. People will sit in small groups and be still. They begin to notice what they are thinking and feeling. It is only by being aware of the thoughts and feelings that arise that one can notice any change in those thoughts or feelings.

Through awareness and the open, compassionate heart, it is possible to support others in the release of certain charges they may hold in their system. When that release occurs, an effect similar to that when a pebble that has been dropped into a still pond creates an outward rippling effect, which changes, for a moment, the surface of the water. Instead of water ripples, there are emotional ripples, changing, for a moment, the energy in the space. A signal has been released or transmitted containing information which we interpret as an emotion. This rippling of an emotion affects the state of the immediate environment for a moment in time. If the others in the group are quiet enough and have developed the ability to observe, then they will notice this change in their environment—a brief change, so they have to be very mindful.

When the ripple of emotion being discharged passes through the awareness of the observers, each individual will experience a momentary change in what they are feeling. Often, at least 60% of the observers will experience the same emotion as the individual being "cleared." For most of the observers, this information simply passes through their awareness leaving little or no trace of its existence. For a few of the observers, this emotional charge may resonate with a charge they hold in their own body/personality. When this happens, the individual experiencing it may have a strong reaction to the information, and we will look at the reasons for this in more detail later. The point of this exercise is to show that not only are we all capable of receiving energetic transmissions from others, as others can receive transmissions from us, but that much of the information we identify with originated outside of the body and consequently is not ours. The body, being an electrical field, transmits and receives information to and from everything in its environment.

Without this understanding, it is easy to see how and why people associate with every thought or feeling that arises in their awareness. Yet when we see, through the little exercise above, that we are picking up on the emotional energy of others, the line between what is mine and what is not gets a little blurred.

If I were in a room with other people, one of whom was feeling nauseous, it is likely that, on some level, they are transmitting that feeling of nausea, usually without any awareness that they are doing so. If circumstances were conducive, then I might pick up on that transmission and feel the nausea as well. If I did not know better, I might think, "Oh! I feel nauseous." If I held that thought, my brain would make certain connections associated with nausea, and the chemicals of nausea would be released into my body. The outcome is obvious, I would truly be feeling nauseous. Knowing of the possibility that this feeling of nausea may have nothing to do with me, but rather that it is an energetic transmission, I am better empowered to stop following the thought and stop creating more nausea-producing chemicals. Don't dismiss this because of the simplicity of the process, try it first and then decide.

Several years ago, I was at an hotel in Austria to give a talk. People from the conference were moving about, unpacking books, etc, and I was talking to the owner of the company. All of a sudden, I felt a pain in my back, quite sharp, I said to the owner, someone in the room has back problems. He called out to everyone in the room, asking who had a pain in their back. One man, who had just recently entered the room acknowledged he had back pain and came over to us. Much to his relief, we were able to ease a lot of the pain. The main point though is that I felt the pain of another. Had I not had the training and awareness,it would have been so easy for me to identify with the back pain. As I think, so I become. And before too long, I have a pain in my back, it becomes real to me, and the more energy I give it, the more real it becomes.

To varying degrees, we are all doing this all the time— picking up on the transmissions from the earth, from electrical fields, from others in our vicinity, and even from others far away. Most of the time, we are quite self-absorbed and lost in our own world and so, fail to notice what is happening around us. We are, on a subconscious level picking up and identifying with many of the transmissions coming from all around us. Even many of those more sensitive people may not totally understand what is happening to them. The auto-immune system seems to take care of a lot of information that is constantly bombarding our energetic field, so we do not notice how we are being impacted by the external environment. Not, that is, until something compromises the immune system. When the immune system starts to struggle, then the external information begins to have a more noticeable, significant impact upon our physical, mental, and emotional state.

Yet this sea of information, this quantum soup that we live in is ever-present and is full of various transmissions from our energetic environment. We are being influenced, often quite subtly, 24 hours a day by the information in this soup that is our world. When we take any particular transmission and identify with it, we have taken a step toward physically becoming that thought or feeling. Many symptoms experienced by individuals were never theirs to begin with, but by identifying with them, they became theirs. A thought or an emotion is not necessarily yours, it is just a thought or an emotion and will remain so until you lay claim to it and identify with it. Then that thought or emotion, by association, becomes your thought or emotion. The more you identify with it, the more it becomes yours; this perpetuates the neural connection, which continues producing more of the same amino acids, flooding the body, and making the feeling more "real."

The more we associate with certain thoughts and feelings the more likely we are to establish what appear to be permanent neural links. Whenever we identify with a particular thought or feeling we are training our brain to form certain neural connections. Once we have these semi-permanent neural connections, every time a certain stimulus enters our awareness in the future, the neural network makes the immediate, familiar connection, based on past behaviour and expectations. So instead of responding to the situation, we go into a standard reaction. While this is a very common part of how human beings are conditioned in this time and age, it is not necessarily the best way to approach life.

Without realizing it, we are associating or identifying with a huge amount of information that our environment, including the people in it, is constantly transmitting to us—much like radio waves. And we are conditioned to react to much of that information.

Neuroscientists tell us, however, that the conscious mind is responsible for as little as 5% of cognitive activity throughout the day, while the other 95% of our behavior arises from the subconscious.

If this is true, then any decisions based on what we imagine to be free will are limited to the 5% of consciousness that is under our control. We may believe we have freedom of choice in most situations of our lives, but this is only because we are operating from a limited place that does not perceive itself as 5% but as 100%. We imagine that we are acting consciously at all times, yet, we are apparently going through life in a predominately unconscious way.

How does the subconscious get all this power?

The charge I mentioned earlier is a product of many things and often ends up in the subconscious. Any information that falls outside of a predetermined, evolving range that we have judged as safe, acceptable, and comfortable gets relegated to the subconscious where it then establishes itself and sets up patterning and possibly neural connections without our conscious knowledge. This is an important piece of the puzzle that we will explore in more detail later.

When we realize that each and every person alive today is sending out transmissions of who they perceive themselves to be, it is not so difficult to understand where all the thoughts or feelings come from that we are at risk of identifying with. As people have identified with various thoughts and feelings in the past, they have become a product of these thoughts and feelings. The more we have identified with these thoughts or feelings, the stronger the transmission that we send, thus perpetuating the cycle of old conditioning.

This is not to say that all thoughts and feelings are just floating around in space, waiting for us to identify with them. Although that may not be very far from the truth. Looking back at the creation of the human body through the prism of genetics and soul memory, we can see that the foundation for our own life's experiences already has various built-in judgments. The nature of that foundation is to personalize the thoughts and feelings that pass through its awareness. The memory that we are calling the journey of the soul would thus have its own agenda, its own likes and dislikes.

It could be correct to say that at birth the body has coding within it that will attract or more easily resonate with particular transmissions from its environment. This is another step to understanding the difference between people—why some are more, or less, sensitive to certain energies or information than others. Why people are drawn to particular ways of being. The unique coding of the individual combines into a complex transmission. This transmission then resonates with identical individual or collective frequencies in its environment which, in turn, feed back what must appear to be a confirmation of the original transmissions validity.

After untold years of noticing certain information that arises in our awareness—rejecting some, identifying with other parts—we can become quite limited. We tend to be able to hear or see only that which fits into who and what we believe ourselves to be at any given moment in our history. It is as though by identifying with a particular thought or belief we establish a particular neural connection, which does not allow us to see other possibilities. We cannot even entertain the thought that other possibilities exist because the established neural connection kicks in so quickly that there is no time to even contemplate choice.

This view may go a long way to explaining how personality develops over time, becoming more and more established, more and more entrenched. It may also help explain how the body can develop various states of dis-ease. If we truly are responsible for manufacturing various chemicals, each associated with a particular emotion, then it is not a great leap of the imagination to see how those chemicals are affecting our physical, mental, and emotional health.

This becomes even more obvious as we explore Dr. Pert's findings more deeply. It is now accepted by many that the amino acids produced by various stimuli to the brain flood the body and seek out receptor sites on the cells of the body, "fitting" onto those cells like pieces of a jigsaw puzzle. The amino acid associated, for example, with anger locates a suitable receptor for itself, keys in, and unlocks the cell, allowing information associated with that amino acid to pass into the cell. When we continually flood our physical system with particular amino acids, the building blocks of life, the cells become accustomed to those amino acids.

It has been observed that when a cell has been bombarded by specific amino acids, it becomes so dependent on—or familiar with—these particular amino acids that when it divides, the sister cell has more receptor sites on it for the amino acid that has been dominating the system. With the continual sub-division of cells, all creating more and more receptor sites for a particular amino acid, the entire body is becoming dependent upon—or perhaps even addicted to—one amino acid over others.

This has the effect of closing down the body's ability to absorb healthy, life-supporting amino acids, which then has a negative impact upon the health of the individual. Even greater support for the concept of, "as we think, so we become."

If we identify with anger, the body will become a manifestation of that anger. If we do this long enough, often enough, then the body will easily and instantaneously return to the energetic place of anger, leaving us, with no apparent control over our response/reaction. We become a victim to a neural web connection. This connection may or may not have been created by us personally. It may be a product of our genetic inheritance. However, it is my belief that, given enough time and association with various thoughts, beliefs, or concepts, the body can become those thoughts, beliefs, or concepts. This might not happen in an overt, obvious way, but it takes place subtly in the energy the body transmits and in what it attracts or identifies with.

Understanding this, we can see how our conditioned reaction to identify and associate with information comes from that 95% of our consciousness that is uncontrollable but actually in control.

If the emotion that appears to dominate a person is not the problem, but the continual identification with that emotion in the past is the real issue, this may offer us a new way of looking at the psychology of the individual. As we think, so we become. However, much of our thinking process appears to manifest from the subconscious, so we may not be in control of it as much as we would like to believe.

The impact this understanding has upon the reality that we are creating is enormous. For we should remember that this is not purely an internal event, not contained within or limited to the body that is producing the chemicals. Rather, through electrical transmission, the body is sending out signals to the world. And interestingly enough, the world responds.

I was working with a young man in Australia many years ago, who had a great deal of anger within him. He had been able to suppress some of it, but he was still subject to violent outbursts, so that his parents-in-law were quite concerned for the health and well-being of his daughters.

During the consultation, he told me he saw people fighting everywhere he went—in the pub, on the street corner, in the store. Everywhere he would go, he would see people fighting. I commented that it must be a very interesting reality that he lived in. I added that I didn't see people fighting everywhere I went. He said, "But you must. This happens everywhere!" I replied, "It happens everywhere in your world, not in mine."

Why did he see people fighting all the time? Do you? Why don't I?

As a result of working in this field for many years, I have discovered that we attract the experiences in life that reflect what we are. But this young man may have never made that connection. He was lost in a drama and was identifying with it, but that doesn't alter the fact that he was witnessing an unusual amount of violence. Why him? We may say that he lived the life style that included such violence, but that is too simplistic. After all, he was happily married with two young daughters, and he was not out prowling the streets late at night looking for trouble.

This man may have inherited the characteristics of violence from his parents, it may have been some troubling soul memory, he may have had experiences as a child that left him really angry. The point I am making here is that it is not important where the anger came from. Suffice it to say he was an angry man. His anger, consciously or otherwise was radiating out from him, like the pebble in the pond. This anger may have drawn him into angry situations, it may even have created the angry situations, or, anger and violence may have been drawn to him. It has been said that we are like magnets attracting to us that which we are.

This is another area that could fall outside the limits of acceptance of many people, yet if you start looking, without judgment or expectations, then you will likely see very similar things occurring. On some level, this young man was creating his personal worldview by putting the total package of who he was into the quantum soup of consciousness. He was experiencing his external reality as a result of certain internal, subconscious beliefs that he held. If indeed this is how things work, it is hard to understand why anyone would create conflict and abuse, pain and suffering. However, if we view it from the perspective that much of our reality is created by the subconscious it is easy to see why and how we create the realities we do.

If the majority of people alive today were to stop creating their world based on their subconscious, the world would be a very different place. But it isn't, and it isn't that simple either.

As we identify with experiences, we tend to judge those experiences as either good or bad. We try to avoid the bad ones in the future, or shut away the memories of them—out of sight, out of mind. As for the good ones, we seem to be on an eternal search for more of those.

The angry young man may have been born with his violent feelings and as such may never have been given the choice to accept or reject them. At least that was how it appeared to him. Anyone else caught up in situations that they have no clear recollection of creating in the first place would feel the same—as helpless victims of circumstances beyond their control. If they ever considered it, they might think themselves a victim of a past that was not theirs and would thus feel powerless to change that patterning.

Yet it is only by the continual identification with all the thoughts and feelings that arise in our awareness, and the judging of all those thoughts and feelings that we remain caught in that never-ending cycle, always trying to deny or make sense of what is happening to and around us.

As children grow, they follow their parents' example—not necessarily following the life of the parents but following their ways of dealing with life's situations. They learn from their parents and others close by to reinforce the patterns they were born with and add to those patterns by their own conditioned reactions. This behavior is so commonplace that it is accepted as a natural part of human conditioning and remains unquestioned.

If any child experiences trauma or any event or situation that overwhelms them, how do they cope? What survival mechanism do they employ to help them through the trauma? I think one common way is to deny the experience—to shut it out, to run away. When anyone, but especially a young child, is faced with a situation that is not just uncomfortable but unbearable, denial is a valuable tool to help them survive what they perceive to be a very hostile environment. Denial is not really a long-term solution to any of our problems, but a quick fix. Unfortunately, if the need arises in childhood to develop such survival skills, those skills don't easily leave us as we mature and get stronger, physically and emotionally.

We are very much creatures of habit, and once we have discovered that a particular skill works for us then we tend to stick with that skill whenever the situation seems to call for it. This is a learned behavior pattern that keeps us from re-inventing the wheel every moment of our day. What worked for us in the past still works in the present. There are many times when this learned skill is very useful in our lives because we just drop into an automatic response as various situations present themselves.

Conditioned reaction, however, may not always be the best way to deal with situations in our lives because it prevents us from truly responding to what is happening to us. If our learned behaviour means that we are locked into one way of seeing a situation, we will appear stubborn or dogmatic to those around us. Our adherence to our single-minded point of view will add to or create tension in our environment, which, perversely, will strengthen our perception even more, which only adds additional tension.

The learned behavior patterns will also limit our perception and thinking process so that we only hear what we expect to hear, see what we expect to see. Consequently, our learned behavior pattern, which caused us to see and hear a certain way, is further justified. In our minds, it is the only way things can be.

This realization is important, if new findings about how reality is perceived are true. We will be speaking more of that later.

Our habit has become so ingrained that we may not be aware that we are still employing denial to help us deal with the day-to-day challenges of life. After all, it's a wonderful coping mechanism. Denial of certain thoughts, feelings, and situations has become so much a part of who we are that the situations that provoke or stimulate the need to deny have been relegated to the subconscious. We no longer have any control over that which we have denied. Denial may have been necessary for a young child, but denial can have its dark side, too.

Imagine a child needing to block out a memory, which does not just go away, but remains in the child's subconscious. Depending upon the intensity of the memory, it may play a significant part in how that person deals with similar situations later in life, when they may not even be aware of how or why they are reacting so strongly because they cannot recall the event that caused them to close down in the first place. They have become a victim to their past, and the subjugated memory will control many of their future decisions.

Carl Gustav Jung had a word for this hidden part of the self; he called it the shadow. And he believed that it was necessary to bring it to light so that a person's "conscious personality and his Shadow can live together." In his work *Psychology and Religion*, he says:

> "Everyone carries a Shadow, and the less it is embodied in the individual's conscious life, the blacker and denser it is. If an inferiority is conscious, one always has a chance to correct it.... But if it is repressed and isolated from consciousness, it never gets corrected and is liable to burst forth suddenly in a moment of unawareness. At all events, it forms an unconscious snag, thwarting our most well-meant intentions."

For Jung, this process was not a striving for the light but a confrontation with the darkness as this quote from his Alchemical Studies makes clear:

> "Filling the conscious mind with ideal conceptions is a characteristic of Western theosophy, but not

the confrontation with the Shadow and the world of darkness. One does not become enlightened by imagining figures of light, but by making the darkness conscious."

Exercise

What happens when you experience a feeling or an emotion? Practice noticing what you do. See how, by giving this emotion energy in the form of your attention, the emotion grows and becomes more real, more powerful.

Now, the next time you notice an emotion, practice saying to yourself, "This is an emotion. It is not mine, it is just how this body is experiencing life." And then try changing your mind, redirecting your awareness away from the emotion onto something else. See how long the emotion lasts when you stop giving it energy.

You may think this is another form of denial, and, at the moment, you may be right, but with practice it becomes obvious that this is not the case. Instead, we tend to become more available for a broader range of emotions than we were previously.

When you first start this, it may not be easy because we are conditioned to fall into old patterns of association and identification.

Chapter Five
The Shadow and Its Charge

I have taken to calling the shadow the backpack because it's something that can be easily visualized.

Imagine putting memories and experiences that are too painful or that you either have no strength or no time to deal with, into a pack that you carry around with you wherever you go. You keep loading up the backpack and carry it with you through life. Instead of emptying the backpack when you get older, and hopefully wiser, the old survival technique of denial makes it so much easier to simply add more memories and experiences to the backpack. Perhaps you promise yourself that you will deal with all of this load you are carrying tomorrow, when you have more time, when you are feeling stronger, but as we all know, tomorrow never comes. And, the longer we leave the memories, the more difficult to deal with they seem to become.

Denial is not the only factor that will add more load to your backpack; it is just one of many. Identification and judgment of feelings and situations in your life will add charge to the backpack. The concept of the backpack is similar in many ways to Jung's "shadow" and also to the 95% subconscious aspects of the self.

When I said earlier that it is the total package of who we are that transmits the information that goes to create our worldview and the experiences we subsequently have, I included the energy and information contained in the backpack. So the denied parts of the self are just as likely to be attracting experiences as the loved or well integrated parts of the self.

The information in the backpack (shadow) appears, according to Jung, to be contrary to our conscious needs and desires. This has the potential to create internal conflict between the loved side of the Self—the light, the open, the aware—and the hidden or dark side of the Self. We have the positive and the negative, conscious or subconscious preferences that generate the charge that builds inside of us. As mentioned, this can lead to inner conflict, but more often than not denial comes once again to the rescue, and we forget that there is such a part of us known as the shadow.

But forgetting or denying it does not make the shadow go away. We are still very much victims to our past, to those unloved parts of the self, that hidden 95%. As these aspects of the self continue to transmit their various messages out into the world, they attract situations to us which because of their very nature, are much easier to deny or run away from than to face and embrace.

As the "gap" between those aspects of ourselves that we have embraced and those we are still in denial of grows, our physical, mental, and emotional energies suffer. The increased strain of trying to balance these two sides of ourselves takes its toll and is just one more stress factor that the immune system has to deal with. This is made even more complicated because, on a conscious level, we are not aware of the play that is being acted out in our mind, emotions, and physical body.

As the inner conflict builds, it can create weaknesses in the physical, mental, and emotional energies. This weakness may manifest as stress, dis-ease, sickness, frustration, etc. As the manifestation of this inner imbalance becomes stronger, the energy or information that we transmit affects those around us and our physical environment. This affect is generally perceived as being negative.

For the most part, people will remain unaware that they are transmitting stress or that they are the recipients of stressed information. We may be aware to varying degrees that we are stressed. but we may not understand the depth of the impact we are having on our environment and those around us.

It is currently a part of the human condition to either remain very self absorbed. This is the most likely scenario— thinking that the stressed information they are picking up on is theirs. This completes the cycle of neural connection, chemical manufacture of amino acids, and physically becoming that which we thought we were.

I would like to make clear that the self-absorption I refer to is not the same as selfishness. One may be self absorbed and still be caring and supportive of others. I am referring to the model that most people subscribe to of the self being the body, mind, and emotions.

We may not understand that the strain we are putting on our physical body may be caused by denying various aspects of our experience as such. For the most part, we have not been made aware that the baggage we carry could be responsible for our health issues. We tend to look elsewhere and often externalize the cause for any imbalance that manifests.

There are many signs and many causes of a body out of balance. We cannot always lay responsibility for ill health, misfortune, unhappiness on the information stored in the backpack. The backpack may only represent a small part of the hidden 95%, which seems to rule our lives. If we, correctly or not, just lump everything in the 95% together and call it shadow for the time being, it may make clearer the degree that we are affected by information that we are no longer conscious of. The shadow side is affecting the lives of everyone on the planet in such fundamental ways that, until we begin to acknowledge the power this aspect of us has, we will continue to create out of very limited awareness and have to deal with the collective creation from that very limited place. Unfortunately, by its very nature, denial, which created the charge in the backpack, precludes the very existence of the shadow/backpack.

Why are some people prone to sickness to accidents, to "bad" luck and not others? Why do some people survive a negative diagnosis and not others? Is life a lottery, or is there something going on that we have just not yet seen? It is fairly obvious that physically manifesting disease is often attributable to some inner physical imbalance in the body, but what caused the inner imbalance to manifest in the first place? I think the information that we store in the backpack can help explain this.

We do not have to believe in soul memory, past lives, or karma to believe in the existence of the shadow. Although, the better we have developed the art of denial, the more difficult it is for us to realize we have a shadow side at all. Remember, though denial is not the cause of the shadow, the fact that possibly up to 95% of our worldview is created subconsciously may have something to do with why we deny information, feelings, and thoughts in the first place.

The conflict that exists between the conscious part of ourselves and the denied or shadow part is transmitted out, affecting not only others around us, but also the environment. We create imbalance in our surroundings, which then supports our belief that we are our thoughts and our feelings.

Individual levels of internal conflict differ, of course. Some people are more at peace with themselves than others. Though again, denial prevents recognition and acceptance of the shadow. Some people may have a sense that something beyond their control is affecting their inner health and the health of their environment, but they struggle with what that is and how to do anything to change the manifesting reality.

This way of looking at the relationship we have with our environment is not something that is readily or easily accepted in the minds of most. We may have accessed parts of this awareness, this knowing individually and independently, but the challenge is to find a way that makes sense of our knowings and gives us a path to follow in order to deepen that understanding.

Earlier, I used the word "charge" to indicate some memory that still had some kind of control over us. We are all our memories, and it is important that we see that. Memory in the form of genetic information, memory in the form of the soul's remembered experiences. Memory is what makes us who we are, whoever that may be, and, without it, we may well cease to be. Memory is important. I think the question that we should be asking ourselves is to what degree we are victims to our memories. If we explore the idea that certain memories hold more charge for us than others, we can see how an intense memory may influence or dictate certain reactions in our life.

Here is a personal story that demonstrates this principle.

Ever since I can remember I have had personal issues with authority. I did not feel comfortable around authority figures, and I certainly did not enjoy being told what to do by people who, themselves, did not know what was going on. In my workshops, I have found out that I am not alone. In fact, when I ask people if they have similar issues, the majority of people in the room laugh and raise their hands, as though I were being pretty stupid to even ask the question. It seems as though a lot of people have trouble with authority. Why is this the case?

I know, from my own experience, that I have no reason to be uncomfortable with authority, as there is nothing in my past that I know of that could justify such a reaction. I am pretty sure that there is nothing in the past of the majority of people in workshops who feel the same way to give them reason for such a strong reaction. Yet it is there, undeniably, actively present in some part of me.

In the past few years, I have had to do a lot of traveling associated with my teaching workshops around the world. In late 1999, I made the United States home. This, of course, meant a lot of traveling into and out of the States. My issues with authority would manifest as quite obvious anxiety, which was always triggered coming through U.S. Customs and Immigration. If you have ever experienced anxiety, you will know the symptoms—a general feeling of discomfort, tightening of the stomach muscles, perspiring, cold and sweaty hands, overall not a pleasant feeling. And this would happen, totally out of my control, every time I entered the States.

Why was I reacting so strongly? I had done nothing wrong, and there was no reason for me to go into such a strong reaction. Why was this happening to me? Was it something my parents had handed down to me through genetic memory? If so, then there were a heck of a lot of parents of workshop participants all around the world, who had handed down the same feeling to their children. That's pretty weird.

Or was this a case of soul memory? And if so, does everyone have this soul memory? Certainly there are many people that appear to, although I am sure there are many people who do not have this sort of reaction to authority. Is it some sort of extreme sensitivity that allows this feeling to manifest and be so overwhelming? This may well be the case. We have noticed in workshops that the more sensitive people are, the more they are at the mercy of those sensitivities and challenged by the energy or information from others and from their environment. So much so that their sensitivity seems to be out of control. But why are some people so much more sensitive than others?

And why me? For those who believe in past lives, it is easy to imagine dozens of labels or reasons, and persecution in a past life is a common one. For people who believe in past lives, memories of persecution are common—too common, I think. But blaming a past life is a possible explanation when all else fails.

As I mentioned earlier, trying to discover the prime cause for any condition is almost impossible and ultimately futile. Forgetting about soul memory for the moment and concentrating on genetic memory as a possible source for certain characteristics—mental, physical, and emotional—how far back does that trail go? How far back do you think you need to go to understand who you are? The big bang? Because I never really expected to be able to work out why I was reacting to authority so strongly, I did not bother even trying. I just accepted that this was happening to me.

In the workshops I use tuning forks to demonstrate the principle of sympathetic resonance and how various "packets" of information can trigger a reaction of other similar packets of information. If we look at any particular piece of information as having a unique frequency, we can see how, and why, this experiment works. We know sound has frequency, colors have frequency, the visible and invisible spectrums of light from the sun are frequencies, X-rays are frequencies, as are microwaves and gamma rays. Even the cells in the human body have unique frequencies. Everything, including taste, smells, feelings, and thoughts have frequencies. The human aura is a transmission of the frequencies of the body, both its integrated and shadow aspects. Solid matter has frequencies. Energy can be seen to have either a frequency or be made up of particles, as the newest physics research has discovered. It is not such a leap to see that information stored in the backpack or even in the physical body has its own unique range of frequencies.

Take two tuning forks, each tuned to exactly the same frequency and hold one of them against a sheet of glass, this only works with tuning forks of certain frequencies. I use C, which is tuned to 649.3 cycles per second. You may find some frequencies work better on wood. Strike the other tuning fork, also C at 649.3 cps so that it vibrates, then hold it against the sheet of glass near the original tuning fork. The glass transmits and amplifies the sound. Take the second tuning fork away from the glass and the remaining, original tuning fork can be heard, even though it was the other tuning fork you struck. This is sympathetic resonance. It happens to pianos in close proximity to each other; as one string is struck, the identical note on the other piano starts to vibrate. Fishermen with two outboard motors on their boat know better than to have both motors running at exactly the same number of revolutions per minute, the motors are likely to self destruct if this happens.

On a human scale, though, what happens when we tune into or come into the proximity of certain information or certain frequencies is that the corresponding part of who we are—physical, emotional, or mental plane—begins to resonate as it is triggered by the other frequency. Without going into detail about the role the heart plays—that comes later—it is difficult to comprehend fully how and why the body reacts to certain frequencies as it does.

Depending upon an individual's sensitivity and ability to notice what is happening to the body, which naturally depends upon the intensity of the information being transmitted, our body may react. Whether we notice it or not, it is happening.

Most people do not recognize that this is happening. This is partly because we are not used to understanding energetic exchange in this way and partly because we are busily self-absorbed. Even if we did notice a change in how we were feeling, we are conditioned to attribute it to something else, something we feel comfortable or familiar with. Many of us are so locked into particular ways of dealing with life that we do not notice the subtle shifts in the energy around us. We often fail to notice the more powerful changes in our environment because the information that we are picking up on is outside of our range of experience and therefore does not register in our awareness. Just because we do not notice the change in how we feel does not mean that it is not happening.

We are most likely to notice a reaction if the particular frequency that we are "receiving" corresponds to some information stored in our backpack or elsewhere in the subconscious. It is as though the energy or frequency of information that we have either connected to or come into close proximity to is pushing an old button on an issue or feeling that still carries a lot for charge for us.

If this issue or feeling is a part of the denied self, something we have felt strongly about in the past and buried long ago because of our inability to look at it, then the triggering of this memory can be quite powerful—even unpleasant. Remember the neural connections that we make by habitually associating with various thoughts and feelings, and the flood of chemicals that is created as a result of this neural link. We can imagine, if the chemicals/amino acids created were judged by us as unpleasant or were actually unhealthy, then we would try and deny that connection to prevent our having to experience those chemicals in the body.

For some of the time, we may well be able to contain or limit the effects of any reaction by using the 5% of consciousness that appears to have some control. If the information we are picking up on, whatever the source, is triggering something held in the subconscious, then we may react physically, mentally, or emotionally, but we do so without any understanding that we are indeed reacting, and we have no control over that reaction. We appear to be complete victims of our subconscious and the shadow that is hidden within it.

If any neural connection is well established, it is going to leave little or no time for us to make any decision on how we respond to certain situations. If this is the case, when the body encounters a particular frequency that reminds it of something from its past, that frequency triggers the neurons associated with that memory. This electrical stimulation creates and releases the amino acids associated with that memory into the body. When this happens, we are likely to get an immediate physiological reaction associated with that memory or experience.

Often the flood of amino acids is so powerful and intense that there is no time to step back and respond to the situation; we go straight into conditioned reactive mode—not just neurologically, but physiologically as well. The body becomes the feeling, and it is as though we are reliving the past. This change in how the body feels, especially when we perceive the change as unpleasant, takes us out of our "comfort zone" and invariably puts us in a defensive state of mind. This is a common reaction when our internal balance is upset.

Throughout the many workshops I have presented, and life experiences in general, it becomes increasingly obvious to me how we react when we are not feeling safe.

Inside, we have certain limits that we are comfortable with, and there are certain no-go areas, where we feel very uncomfortable. We can refer to this as our comfort zone. While we are inside that zone, everything is fine, and life is good. The moment we are taken out of that zone, the world becomes an unfamiliar, threatening place that may remind us of trauma from our past. Most likely the subconscious has been awakened, and we are feeling very lost.

What takes us out of the comfort zone is information or situations that are outside of our control, and when we have no control, we react. The form that reaction takes depends upon who is reacting and the degree to which that person perceives himself/herself to be out of control.

I have noticed this reaction can follow certain patterns. First, the person becomes mildly agitated, or perhaps embarrassed. They may become anxious. Remember that these feelings are created by the chemicals associated with stress, and identifying with anxiety is making the feelings very real to the person experiencing it. So the person is actually becoming the feelings that have been stimulated by a word, a memory, a particular situation. After the agitation comes the need for defensiveness and—if this does not allow the person to control the situation—aggression.

I have observed this pattern more in men than women, who react differently to being taken out of their comfort zones. But we all react when we are feeling unsafe. The feelings we are referring to here though are no longer "real"; they are just memories that are being triggered and brought once again into the light. We will see that it is not the memories themselves that are the problem, but rather the fact that we have no control over them. The key to change lies in developing the ability to change how we react to all of the various stimuli we are subject to.

The triggering of a memory does not have to be an uncomfortable experience. In fact, for the most part, we are reminded of things that gave us pleasure in the past. However, this can be just as much an "out of control" event as being reminded of painful memories. We tend to seek the good and deny the bad; this is human nature. But this simple judgment will keep us prisoners of our desire, always polarized and never finding balance.

When we are reminded of any charge we hold in our shadow or subconscious, there are various levels of reaction depending upon the intensity of the memory. The more we have tried to run away from or deny any part of ourself, the more charge builds up around that memory. The stronger the charge, the more likely we are to be powerless against the flood of chemicals and the associated physiological reaction. We can lose the ability to be rational until we can stop producing those particular chemicals. Once the production of chemicals returns to something more familiar, more inside of our comfort zone, we could say that we get back in control of ourselves again. If there had been no charge held in the backpack, we could never have "lost" control of ourselves in the first place.

There are, of course, varying degrees of this type of reaction. It is not always all consuming, but most often, it is only a minor embarrassment, for example, you may feel your face get red. Even something so simple as embarrassment can lead to a more uncomfortable state if given the energy. I can remember, years ago, being easily embarrassed, taken quickly out of the very narrow confines of my comfort zone.

When I felt my skin begin to flush, I would think, "oh no, this is not good." Everyone could see my embarrassment, and if you are even remotely self-conscious, this is not a good place to be. I did not stop and say to myself, "oh, I have just stepped out of my comfort zone and this is the way I react." Instead I said, "this is really bad," thus taking the feeling very seriously. The more seriously I took the feeling, the more red I became, the more red I became, the more uncomfortable I got. And if the people around you were of a mind, they could make it so much worse. Kids are good at that.

I still get embarrassed and feel myself flushing, but not so easily or quickly now. My comfort zone has expanded considerably as a result of practicing this way of being. Now when I feel myself going red I can say, "ah, the comfort zone is just being stretched, no big deal." I can be with the feeling without getting lost in the feeling. This is a very important thing to be able to do. It is very liberating.

It was much the same with my issues with authority. For whatever reason, I was easily triggered into an anxious state when confronted by authority. Obviously, it was something way outside of my comfort zone. Was it a memory of mine? Of my ancestors? Was it some soul memory? Or was it something completely unrelated to authority? Another sensitivity on my part that was triggered by a feeling?

Or was it something real, some energy that is found in the line of people waiting to be processed through Customs and Immigration? Or was it a combination of many factors?

I think it was probably a combination of things all coming together and triggering the feeling of anxiety in me. Trying to find the cause is futile, as there are so many possibilities, and we would only settle on the one we felt to be true at the time anyway, as the answer that fits into our current way of seeing things. Assuming you found an "answer" you felt comfortable with, it is not necessarily going to help you overcome getting lost in the feeling of anxiety.

There were times for me when this feeling was quite overpowering and uncomfortable. I grew tired of being a victim to anxiety, especially since I had nothing to hide or be ashamed of. I recognized that I was being triggered, but the charge held in the shadow or subconscious was so strong that I had no control over it. Every time I was reminded of this feeling, by the rush of chemicals in my body, it was too late to do anything about it. I had immediately gone into reaction, without a moment to consider what was happening. I needed to break the cycle before the chemicals took control and I got lost, once again, in anxiety. I was being taken, big time, out of my comfort zone and was powerless to do anything about it.

There are many times we may feel anxiety, and we are justified in feeling it, as certain situations may support certain feelings. But when we feel something, and there is no real reason for us to feel that way, then we should know that it is something inside of us that is calling out for attention.

My issues, whatever they are, may be unrelated to authority. I could be holding charge around various memories, which are triggered by the frequencies associated with authority. Some people, when they hear a piece of music may have fond memories that they associate with that music, the good memory being triggered by the frequencies. Other people may have a negative reaction to that music. It could remind them of an unpleasant event in their lives. Others may not associate that particular piece of music with any memory. It is the same music, we just have different ways of reacting or responding to the sounds. So each of us, with our very unique backgrounds, personalities, and shadows reacts differently to information.

One way that we can take more control of our lives is to accustom ourselves to stop identifying so strongly with any thoughts or feelings that arise in our awareness. As I mentioned earlier, human conditioning being what it is, our tendency is to identify and associate with, and personalize everything that arises in our awareness. This is my thought, this is my feeling. I am thinking this, I am feeling that.

Because this has been how human beings have known themselves and gained a sense of identity throughout the ages because this is how it has always been done, we have simply picked up the baton and just kept running with it. We rarely stop to question such a fundamental issue, assuming instead that it is true, and then, from within that assumption, we try and understand who we are. For those who do begin to question their very nature, many alternative ways of thinking are available, but most of them are still based in the original perception that you are your thoughts and your feelings.

Many thinkers and philosophers throughout history have offered us clues to the way out of this hamster wheel of life, yet few seem to have heard and fewer still seem to have taken those words to heart. I realize it is not possible for me, sitting here at the computer in the first months of 2006 to really know who took what seriously and when. All I can do is to look at where the world is now, see the base upon which most people build their lives, see what is important for people and compare that with the teachings of the "masters." There may be vast numbers of people who listened to the words of the Buddha, of Jesus, of Mohammed, and of others who could see clearly. All of those people may have reached an enlightened state, but as that enlightened state does not seem to be the dominant reality on the planet at the moment, I really cannot tell.

Exercise

Are there any parts of your life that seem to be outside of your control? Do you wonder why things happen to you and not others? Is life fair to you?

The next time a situation arises that challenges you, try stepping back for a moment. Acknowledge the emotion, and say to yourself that this is simply how your body is reacting to external stimuli or buried memory, and repeat that it is not yours. Breathe through the emotion and watch it disappear.

Again, this will take time to master, but with perseverance it gets easier each time you try it. As you get better at this, notice also how it affects those around you who were previously caught up in the emotion of the moment as well.

Chapter Six
Identifying with Our Thoughts and Feelings

We have looked at the mechanism where identification with a thought or feeling creates a physical response to that thought or feeling. We have explored how that process can create the reality of who you perceive yourself to be. Thoughts or feelings—both the ones you think of as yours and the ones that surround you—are for the most part simply energetic transmissions. These are generated by each and everyone of us. The degree that we have personalized or identified with thoughts and feelings in the past will influence the intensity of the transmission.

We have also looked at the process where the more we believe a thought or feeling to be ours, the more it becomes ours, and the more it becomes ours, the more powerful the transmission. It is no wonder we have trouble trying to find any original cause, as we are lost in a sea of thoughts and feelings, all vying for our attention. And we continue to keep taking all of those thoughts and feelings so personally.

Stopping this process poses challenges, not the least of which is that this is the most commonly held belief on the planet and going against it is to further isolate yourself. Not a popular path to travel.

We have seen how those thoughts, feelings, and belief patterns we have believed to be ours in the past have established what appear to be fixed neural connections. To some degree or other, we are all in this established reality, and it is hard enough to dismantle even when you know you are in it. And if you don't even know you are in it, how can you be objective enough to recognize what is going on?

If we can step back far enough for a moment, we may see that the thoughts and feelings we are experiencing are not ours until we claim them, take them personally, take them seriously, identify with them. The idea that we are not our thoughts and feelings may appear to be such a totally new way of looking at our relationship to ourselves, that, at first (and even at second glance) many people simply cannot imagine this to be true. Yet with practice, as thousands of people have found, it is indeed this way, and once you realize it and put it into practice, the results are very liberating indeed.

This information is not new—in fact, it is very old. It is just that when it was introduced, human nature, lost within its personal drama, distorted the information. We are so conditioned into one way of being that we cannot even consider the possibility that anything can be so simple, especially in a world where we always look outside for the answers and where individuals are more than happy to give away personal power to others.

In order to not identify with the thoughts and feelings that arise, it helps if we stop taking ourselves quite so seriously—a major challenge for many of us. If we can reduce the amount of judgment we have around certain thoughts or ways of being, it helps the process along. "Judge not lest you be judged."

These three things may be the most powerful ways we can change our lives, and also—when we first try—the most difficult to do.

It is our association with and judgment of thoughts and feelings that keeps us a virtual prisoner to our past. My association with anxiety was certainly keeping me a prisoner of that emotion.

Remember, anxiety is not the problem. It is the continued identification with anxiety that is the problem.

Having decided to change my relationship to anxiety, I worked on clearing or releasing any charge I was holding on to around anxiety or authority—the charge that seemed to trigger the memory and the chemicals.

While I did this with an awareness of the feelings of anxiety, I did not limit myself to working on any specific feeling—in this case, anxiety. I was more concerned with changing my relationship with anxiety, and, in order to do that, I needed to practice becoming more mindful of how I was feeling at any given time. When I would notice a feeling, I would say to myself, this is such and such a feeling, it is how my body is relating to certain information. It is not my feeling, but how my body is experiencing a particular chemical rush. Previously I would have made this feeling mine by giving it more energy, and I would have done this by saying this is my feeling, thereby reinforcing the neural connection, putting more chemicals associated with that feeling into my body.

The secret to changing the body's reaction is to catch the thought or feeling early enough, before the body is once again lost in the chemical discharge. For many of us, there is no such moment, me and my issues around anxiety, for example. There was no time when I could say, "ah, this is anxiety, it is not mine, just the way the body is reacting to some external (?) information." With practice, I was able to slow down the moment between my body picking up the transmission that would trigger my anxiety and the inevitable rush of chemicals. Catching the feeling early gives us the opportunity to decide whether the feeling is going to take control of us or we of it.

The clearing must have worked because when I returned to the US several years ago, after working at releasing my association with "anxiety" and I passed through Customs and Immigration, I felt no anxiety at all. This was reflected in the welcome I got from the officer who stamped my passport. It was very different to previous times when I had picked up and identified with high levels of anxiety. Of course....

We are all a part of the quantum soup. If I transmit anxiety, then it is going to affect everyone around me to some degree. It may make the people feel uncomfortable, certainly affecting the people working at the immigration booths. If my levels of anxiety had been much higher, the passport officer would have felt so uncomfortable, he might even have assumed I needed further investigation. A self-fulfilling prophecy. I identify with a feeling, in this case anxiety, my body goes into overdrive manufacturing amino acids associated with anxiety, my body becomes very anxious, I transmit anxiety, and those around me pick up on it.

Now, when I return to the US and am waiting my turn to be processed, I still may sense anxiety. I can see this as a reminder of what anxiety feels like. But now I know that it is not mine. I see it for what it is—anxiety being transmitted by someone, somewhere in the customs hall—but it is not mine. Sometimes I can look around and see others who are picking up on the transmission and identifying with it.

They are helping to strengthen the feeling and spreading it around for others, less fortunate than myself, to pick up on and identify with. I still recognize the feeling of anxiety, but I am no longer hard-wired, no longer a victim to a memory or an uncontrollable flood of chemicals in my body. Amazing. It's quite wonderful, of course, to feel anxiety, not judge it as good or bad, but just recognize it as a feeling and let it go. It can be as simple as that.

It is our past that has created who we believe we are today or rather, it is our identification with the experiences in our past. It would be very difficult for most of us to ignore the information that seems to be built into the body when it is born. If we can, for a moment, see that even those memories are a product of how we—or our ancestors—have identified with experiences in the past, then we may have opened a door to allow us to change.

Why would we want to not identify with the body or the personality? This is a valid question. But if there is any part of your personal or collective reality that you are not happy or comfortable with, if there are people in your world who upset you, this may be reason enough to explore your options. It is only by taking a few steps down this path that we can begin to understand the power that is ours when we stop limiting ourselves. This is especially important for those people who feel they are victims to a past they do not understand. It is no less important for each and everyone of us, as it opens us up to a very different future, giving us new tools to work with old information.

Another benefit of this way of being is recognizing how our shadow plays out by creating a significant physiological reaction around anxiety, for example. It should be obvious from this experience that unless we change who we are, or who we believe ourselves to be, we will just get more of the same tomorrow. Had I not seen my periods of anxiety in a different light, one that made it relatively simple to change, I could still be experiencing anxiety in situations where I was confronted by authority.

I think that change is the only constant we can rely on. How and where change takes us is the responsibility of each and every one of us. We cannot rely on others to lead us out of the darkness if they are themselves lost in the darkness.

The methods we use to bring about change need not be so complicated that they appear out of the reach. This may be something we have believed in the past, but that does not make it the truth, or the best—or only—way. Change does not have to be violent. In fact, if violence is involved in change, then it is not change that is happening, but just more of the same, and it will beget more violence in the future.

Change can be so simple and fundamental that we miss the opportunity because we are looking too hard at how we have done things in the past. Many people who seek change in their lives are trying very hard to do something to make life easier for themselves, in other words, they are using the old model based on struggle. It doesn't have to be that way.

By "do something," I mean they are trying to fix something or improve their situation. If people remain unconscious of the role their own issues play in creating their reality, they will forever be caught in the struggle to fix the manifesting issue while not looking at the cause. Whilst we perceive there to be a problem, we are drawn into the place where we must do something to fix the problem. We often fail to see that it is often our relationship to the issue that needs changing. Once we are able to do that, the problem may well disappear.

There may be situations where there is so much energy contained within a problem, so many people involved, so much complexity, that it appears to be more than one person can handle. Nevertheless, the basic issue is the individual's relationship to the information or event. If we don't begin by changing our relationship to what we perceive as the problem, we will remain victims to that event or information throughout our lives.

Perhaps I am being overly ambitious here, thinking to change the world by changing my relationship to it. But we don't have to take on such a huge project as changing the world. Better that we just focus our energies on ourselves or our immediate family and environment. Practice on the little stuff, and the big stuff just may take care of itself.

When I changed my relationship to anxiety, it no longer dominated a part of my experience. I cannot measure the effect my change had on everyone else, but I do know that when I stopped taking the feeling of anxiety seriously, I stopped forwarding the message or feeling of anxiety. Instead of being part of the problem as I was before, I became a part of the solution to the global issue of associating with anxiety. Now, instead of adding to the overall feelings of anxiety in the world, I have learned how to take it into my heart and embrace it without getting lost in it. This has the effect of taking some of the charge out of the feeling in the collective consciousness and, at the same time, not adding charge to my own backpack.

There may be times, of course, when anxiety is appropriate, but I will be able to recognize those moments and differentiate, what is appropriate and what isn't. Previously, I was lost in the feeling and unable to determine whether it was appropriate or not.

Many people try to fix the reality they find ourselves in without even imagining that they could be the problem. This is particularly challenging if the person is sick or in pain. Being able to see that the current feelings are products of the past requires a great ability to be objective about what is happening in the moment. Had a person who is sick or in pain had that ability it is quite possible that the sickness or pain would not have presented in the first place.

There are many other factors that need to be taken into account, but this is just one area that is not often looked at and may hold some answers. This is not a situation of blame where someone has done something wrong. How can anyone do anything wrong when they are subject to so much influence from their subconscious? The hard part, I think, is that if dis-ease is manifesting, and the cause for that dis-ease lies in the denial of some part of the self in the past, then the very situation out of which dis-ease arose blocks any ability to see it, let alone take responsibility for what is manifesting.

I don't believe it is always possible to fix the external by doing something to or about it—and I don't mean that one should do nothing to lessen pain and suffering in this world. This is still a very important part of humanity, yet if we look at who is trying to "fix" the problem, we see a personality—possibly with the best of intentions—but a personality none the less. If we look at the nature of that personality, we will see that it is based on a personal past, with its likes and dislikes, its judgments and prejudices, and certain beliefs it holds true over other beliefs. How can any one personality, coming from such a place, know or appreciate what is best for others. Perhaps an answer is to help others unconditionally, without expectations. Anyone coming from a limited personality that is seeking to create a safe environment for itself might do so by trying to impose its values and beliefs on others, and this invariably leads to conflict as others resent having to adopt someone else's values. There is nothing wrong with trying to create a safe environment, but if it is created at the expense of the safety of others, there can be no lasting safety, and it will take continual effort to maintain any sense of safety that is ultimately doomed to failure at great expense.

Until we change who we are on the inside, I believe that we are not going to change the manifesting reality in any fundamentally positive way because that manifesting reality is just a product of the totality of who we are. As I mentioned earlier, external change is certainly a stimulus for creating internal change, but if we are not feeling safe, then expecting change to last on any worthwhile level is not realistic. To always seek safety by manipulating the external may not be the best way to go. If your search for safety is based on the unexpressed information held in the backpack, you will never find what you seek, for the shadow is always amongst the aspects of the self that you project, and you will never find peace until the shadow has been brought out in the open and embraced.

This can be easier than you might imagine, though when Jung talked about this, he said, "The task of midlife is not to look into the light, but to bring light into the darkness. The latter procedure, however, is disagreeable and therefore not popular." (*Alchemical Studies*, p. 335.) We can see where he was coming from, facing the shadow after a lifetime(s) of running away from it would be pretty daunting—assuming you accept that you have this shadow side in the first place. Yet, if there was a way you could change your relationship to the shadow aspects of the self, then perhaps it would not be so disagreeable after all. I believe this work presents one way to do this—to bring your own shadow into the light of day, understand it for what it is, and move beyond always being a victim to your dark side.

I think it was a wonderful moment, in *Star Wars*, when Darth Vader asked Luke to come to the dark side. Darth Vader was right—unimaginable power lies in the dark side of the force. The danger to Luke and everyone else fighting for the light side would be that Luke would get lost in the dark side. Most of his buddies were lost in the light side, hence the polarization that allowed ongoing conflict. "Real life" isn't that much different. Understanding that light and dark are both different sides of the same coin is the beginning of the self's liberation from this almost self-imposed tyranny—reality that we take for real.

At this point, it becomes obvious that if Luke and his buddies do not fight the dark side, it will overcome all those opposed to it and rule—not a pleasant outlook. Once we have a manifestation of the dark side, however, it can only have come about because of polarisation, which means there is a light side involved. In "real" life, it is not so easy to be objective about any conflict and determine who is the dark and who is the light. Those on team A believe they are in the right, and they may even think they have god on their side, and those on side B think exactly the same way. Just because I was born in one country does not automatically mean that country is on the side of right in any conflict.

When we can embrace both sides of the self, light and dark, neither will ever have power over us again. This is not to suggest that we all go over to the dark side for a few years to try and bring balance back. That is an approach to perceived inequity used by many minority groups in order to be heard and accepted. This polarization or externalization, this expression of suppressed energy adds to the charge held by the majority against the minority and further alienates the minority, until, with persistence, the voice of the minority is gradually accepted into "mainstream." Or not. I am not suggesting that we legitimize any expression of the dark side or condone acts of abuse of any kind. Maybe I am a little too late there, but it seems that the dark side has been having a ball throughout the centuries—the yin and the yang, the light and the dark, the good and the bad in eternal conflict.

The point here is that the dark side is playing out all around us and will continue to do so whilst we have any aspects of ourselves hidden away. The shadow cannot be denied. If we were to embrace the dark side, as Darth Vader suggests, but not lose ourselves in it—and that is the key, to not lose ourselves in it—it would cease to have power over us. Witness my embracing the feeling of anxiety.

If you ever thought about it, you may have considered anxiety a weakness, a part of the shadow self best denied and hidden away. There is an old truism, "what we resist persists." Even if you appear successful in further burying the feelings of anxiety, they will still be there, unresolved, creating inner conflict, that may well manifest one day as a state of physical, mental, or emotional dis-ease.

When you can bring the feeling of anxiety out into the light, see it for what it is (it is just a feeling after all, and feelings are an integral part of who we are), then, with practice, it will cease to have power over you. You may still feel anxious, but you don't have to get lost in anxiety. It is the getting lost in any emotion, particularly in those we judge as negative, that disempowers us. It is getting lost in the dark side that is terrifying for most people, but this fear is often born out of ignorance. We don't truly understand the shadow, so our imagination goes to work and creates a huge monster. In our ignorance, our lack of awareness, we empower the shadow. God and the devil are classic examples of extreme polarization.

In our flight from the dark side we tend to get lost in the light side, which is just as debilitating as getting lost in the dark side. For if, at the expense of our shadow, we seek the light, denying any hidden aspects of self, we continue to create a personal reality that is not in balance. Then we externalize the cause for the imbalance, god and the devil, us and them, the weather, the neighbors, whatever. This is the only way the shadow side can express itself in someone who is still in denial, and remember, denial is not a dirty word, not a judgment of who we are, but just the remnant of a survival mechanism that was important once upon a time.

The more we deny our shadow, the more it seeks balance through expressing itself externally, and the more physically obvious it becomes. This is not anything new, and our "age" is no different from any other "age." History is continually repeating itself, mainly because the players all take themselves and the parts they play so seriously. Looking back over the centuries, you have to wonder sometimes if we will ever learn. The Christians are STILL fighting the Muslims! Or vice versa…

We are born into the body of a baby, and, for the moment, it doesn't matter where we came from, nor does it matter what memories we bring with us. The baby is born into a time and place where everyone takes themselves very seriously. The baby learns from its parents, siblings and environment so, by the time it perceives itself to be separate, the conditioning for "seriousness" is well and truly established and the child conforms to consensus reality. What else can it do? People who are different, in this case, those who do not take themselves seriously, have to learn the art of denial very early on to be able to survive what must appear to them to be a very hostile, very crazy world.

The baby/child learns by example, just as its parents had learned that they are separate, isolated individuals. This may go against the baby's intuitive knowing, but being only a few months old, what do they know? Their personality develops, they are taught right and wrong— which is all relative, of course, as what they are taught depends on who is doing the teaching. Children learn to judge for themselves, they have preferences, they begin making their own decisions. If they have been brought up in anything other than a totally loving environment, there is a good chance they will learn the art of denial. They learn self-worth or self-hatred, they develop self-confidence or learn to blame themselves or others. In short, they learn to become the adults who will eventually take themselves pretty seriously.

Because they are not told otherwise, they believe that the thoughts and feelings they have are theirs, and they learn to express the good ones and deny the bad. They become replicas of previous generations. They may have different dreams, they may even evolve beyond ancestral expectations and limitations, but essentially, they are playing the same old game, with the same old rules. There may be a revolution here and there, but even revolutions play by the same old rules—take yourself seriously and get whatever the personality needs, no matter the cost to others.

Of course, there are many altruistic people out there who care for others more than they care for themselves— wonderful, except they still playing by the same old rules. I am my thoughts, I am my feelings, this is mine, that is yours, and the shadow, well, that has nothing to do with me, that must be yours!

As long as we, as collective humanity, play by the old, very outdated rules, you can guarantee that we will just keep getting more of the same, day in day out, year in year out, millennium in millennium out.

We cannot say that we were not warned, we cannot claim that we have not been given sneak previews of other ways of being. Yet still we persist in playing the same old games over and over again. And you know, perhaps it really does not matter. Perhaps the whole point is to play the game, to get lost in the drama, do whatever it is that you can get away with, hang the consequences, you only live once, right? Have fun, make hay while the sun shines, get as much as you can, as often as you can, kill and be killed ...

Justify your actions, claim you are doing it for the good of the people, for god, for the devil. Just make up some rules so you can sleep at night, and you'll be fine. Maybe.

If I truly believed that, I wouldn't be bothered writing this book. I would be out there partying (or shopping—or whatever) till I dropped. Is my belief that there is something else going on, something else worth discovering about the nature of who we humans really are just a belief?

I understand that I am still lost in the drama of the collective and, as such, really do not know what the heck is happening. Have I just chosen another play? Am I acting another part, equally lost, taking myself and my "world" seriously, even though I am attempting not to? Quite likely. Yet there is something deep down inside me—perhaps it is the intuitive knowing of the baby struggling back to the surface ("… Except as little children shall ye come to me …"). Perhaps, just perhaps, this is a key to the survival of the species, to allow the intuitive knowing of the baby to re-surface. Because of the very process and all the survival skills it takes to get there, growing up into an "adult" of the species often blocks the return to the innocence of the child. And then we get old and die—if we are lucky enough to get old—and then what? Is it all over? Probably not, but we don't know for certain either way.

I remember, a few years ago, waking in the middle of the night and thinking that, in order to continue with my life's work of teaching and sharing this information and to improve my ability to be in relationship, I needed to return to the innocence of the child. This was a powerfully emotional moment for me, and I cried for what seemed like hours, till I eventually fell back to sleep. Why cry? Why get emotional? What is the big deal? The big deal, I think, was that the knowing that the little baby that was once me had made for a very sensitive little child. For whatever reason, whether it was real or imagined, it was very real to the child and that child had what it perceived to be a hard time in its early years.

For three months after this insight, I would occasionally burst into tears for no apparent reason. I did not know exactly what I was processing, but I knew that what was finally coming out were the unshed tears of the child, the pain and hurt, real or imagined, that had been stored up inside of me for many years. I did not need to know the details. It was sufficient to let it happen, knowing that I was letting go of shadow issues. I am not sure how much it helped me be in relationship with myself and others, but it is impossible to imagine what my life would have been like had I not released so much tension. Would I have gotten sick as a result of continuing to hold on to the pain? I do not know and perhaps will never know. But I am glad it was released, and it opened the door for more shadow to come to the surface to be embraced so that I could continue to move beyond it.

Exercise

Are there situations that you struggle with, situations that you are continually trying to correct? How long have you been trying to fix things in your life? And has it made a lot of difference? Are you better off now than you were, or do the old patterns keep returning?

While we try and fix our lives, we remain caught in a cycle of giving energy to that which troubles or disturbs us because we always the thought in mind that by fixing this problem, we will be happy, or wealthy, or in love, or whatever.

Have you ever wondered what would happen if you pretended you were someone else? How would they deal with this situation? Or perhaps if you were someone else, this situation would never bother you in the first place.

If you can change your mind, let go of your expectations and simply open up to the situation and get out of your own way, would things change?

Try this with the less powerful situations first, and work your way up.

Chapter Seven
Journey of the Soul

I particularly like the Tibetan Buddhist description of the journey of the soul. Soul may not be the right word, but it does convey to most people the nature of the essence of the human experience, so, correct word or not, I will use it to represent that part of us which endures.

Imagine that you are more than your body, more than your thoughts, your feelings, your personality. Imagine that there is a part of you that is indeed eternal. For the time being, we can call the eternal aspect of "you" your "soul." We will use words to build the picture, to make this whole concept easier to grasp.

By definition, it follows that if you are eternal, you have always been around and always will be. This is another assumption, which may prove false as we explore this idea in greater depth. Even the simple definition of "you" and whether "you" exist becomes questionable. Who or what is the "you" we are talking about? We currently associate this "you" with the body, the thoughts and feelings that body experiences, the personality. But if you are not the body, the thoughts, feelings or personality, then we are going to have to redefine who "you" are. So, for the time being, we hang that hat on the soul.

You are the soul, having a physical experience, associating with thoughts and feelings, identifying with a personality.

Why you, the soul, is even bothering to have this experience is another question that may or may not get answered to your satisfaction later in the book. The prime cause for you to step into a body in the first place is something that I cannot even pretend to know the answer for. You can always make one up. People have been doing that for millennia, so why stop now!

If the assumption that you are eternal, that you have a soul that endures throughout the ages is correct, then it stands to reason that it has been around a long, long time and will be around for a long, long time yet. We could even associate the word "charge" with the soul, defining it as information and experiences held in the memory of the soul.

Looking back at how the charge between the shadow self and the open, light self creates conflict that seeks to find a balanced state—often looking outside of the self for that balance—then we could imagine the soul is trying to seek balance as well. I expect, however, that there is more to the soul than the attempt to seek some balance. The problem with trying to understand something like the soul is that anything lying outside of our current belief patterns is subject to interpretation by our personality. We have already talked about how the personality can only understand what is within its personal, current worldview. So any talk of the soul is more hypothesis than known fact. But, take your pick—there are many hypotheses out there claiming to be the truth.

According to the Buddhist teachings, when a soul passes into a physical body, it forgets who or what it truly is and associates strongly with the physical form. It becomes the child, with all of the related thoughts and feelings of the child and its environment. It takes itself, as the child, seriously. So we do not know who we are because we forgot this when we became the human being. This "forgetting" would explain why we so strongly identify with the body and the personality.

I can only imagine that not forgetting would equal being born with full memory of the past. If you had a conscious memory of everything from the past, perhaps this would be an enlightened state. If there was no personality through which you filtered your experiences, no shadow that held you victim, no subconscious that was always making up your mind for you, this state might offer a freedom that is currently beyond our ability to comprehend.

That may be our goal—to recover that knowing and the intuitive knowing of the baby. To come into a body remembering your past is not such an easy thing to do.

To some, the possibility that the soul has had more than one experience would validate reincarnation. If reincarnation exists, it certainly lends credence to the concept of soul memory. You may or may not believe in reincarnation. At this point in our journey, I don't think it matters either way. Like many of the concepts in this book, we take and use what we find appropriate, while trying not to get caught up in defending or denying any belief.

The moment you say that something is or is not true, all you are saying is that this is acceptable or not, given your current perceptions and beliefs. Taking a stand on an issue immediately polarizes you—the us-and-them syndrome—

and once again, you get lost in defending the indefensible. It is possible that your time here may be better spent looking beyond all of the for and against arguments.

I am not even sure what I believe about reincarnation. I sense something beyond the immediately visible or knowable, but I do not know what it is (yet). Perhaps each of our lives is a pearl, and all of the lives we have lived are all strung together on a string like pearls. The string may be the soul, linking all manifestations of its desire to experience life in a physical body. But even this image is going to suffer under the microscope as we continually let go of our old perceptions of self. It is a valuable image and serves a purpose, but it is not something to take too seriously—just a tool to be used as long as it may be of help.

As I release my attachment to the body and to thoughts and feelings as being the totality of who I am, my understanding of who I am starts to get very fuzzy round the edges. The safe little hidey hole of the personality, the place where I could hide and feel safe is no longer so small, no longer so safe.

The simple answer of "I am my body, I am my thoughts, my emotions" is gone. I'm not, and I can see that now. I did not set out to dismantle my perceptions of who I was, it just sort of happened along the way. I have not completely lost my attachment to or association with the body, thoughts, and feelings. It is just that I can see more clearly now that any fixed beliefs, rigid thought patterns, or emotions I identified with are not who I am. I am all of them and none of them—they just come and go. This is not easy to explain to someone who still identifies strongly with their personality, their thoughts and emotions.

I think the question we could be asking ourselves is, "Do we have any choice about what memories we can bring in with us? Can we remain conscious and bring all memory with us when we take a new body?" Remember, we are products of our past. And if we continue to react—consciously or subconsciously—as we have in the past, we will get more of the same tomorrow. If we want to develop the ability to retain consciousness through the moment of death and beyond, we need to begin now, changing the programming to allow for a greater possibility in the future.

According to the Buddhists, there are some who do retain memory. The people who achieve this are called boddhisatvas. Boddhisatva means literally "one whose essence is enlightenment," that is, someone who has attained enlightenment but chooses to remain in or return to this world to help others on their path. The majority of us, however, seem to get recycled with no memory prior to the "new" body.

Why do we get recycled anyway?

During the process of associating with and personalizing the body, thoughts, and feelings, we become polarized. This appears to be automatic and is supported by everyone around us, as they have also taken this polarization seriously. Our judgments and preferences, any dogmatic views and prejudices we hold, all born out of the past, create an inner imbalance. This state of imbalance is, in turn, responsible for the development and sustainment of the shadow aspects of self.

This inner imbalance creates a state of conflict in our minds which, as previously mentioned, can manifest either externally or internally as physical, mental, or emotional dis-ease, and this conflict holds a charge much like a battery has a charge, both positive and negative. Neither polarity is good or bad, both are necessary for the battery to be of any use.

It is the same with us. The approximately 95% of our consciousness, of which we are unaware, and even the shadow, which we may run from and deny because of shame or fear, are both valuable parts of who we are. Being free from the shadow involves acknowledging our shadow attributes, accepting them, examining them for greater understanding, and then integrating them back into our awareness of who and what we are. This idea of embracing our shadow has profound significance for each of us because it leads to healing, balance, and wholeness.

So, even though we may feel that our shadow is shameful or consists of unworthy aspects of our being, it is, in reality, quite the opposite. As C.G. Jung says in *Aion*:

> "The shadow is a moral problem that challenges the whole ego-personality, for no one can become conscious of the shadow without considerable moral effort. To become conscious of it involves recognizing the dark aspects of the personality as present and real. This act is the essential condition for any kind of self-knowledge."

And it is knowing the shadow and admitting it openly into our life that gives us control over our lives.

Imagine a test tube, with marks spaced out the length of the tube, each representing 5% of the capacity of the tube. The lower 90% of the tube is dark and murky and represents the subconscious. The next 5%, the zone between the subconscious and the aware, conscious state is cloudy and gray, neither totally dark, nor totally light. The top 5% is clear, representing that part of consciousness we believe to have control over.

The area between the top 5% and the bottom 90% is information that we are aware of but deny. For whatever reason, memory held in this region is judged by us as painful. We know it is there and, for the most part, choose not to do anything about it. We are not even aware of the lower 90%, so, for the time being, we cannot do anything about it. We can, however, develop the ability to work with the information stored in that zone between the aspects of our self we have accepted and those we have denied. As we gradually uncover the shadow and bring it to light our fully conscious self expands into what was once the shadow, creating a reduced shadow percentage. The new fringe, or boundary becomes the area between 85% and 90%, our new gray zone. And so the journey into the true self is underway.

From where we stand now, can we even consider the possibility of being totally conscious? Can we imagine what it would be like to live life no longer the victim of subconscious conditioning? Probably not, but, like any journey, we cannot possibly know of the adventures that await us. All we need to do is take the first step and be open to experience what the journey presents.

Until we take that first step, we continue to avoid dealing with our shadow. The more we run from the shadow, the more charge builds up and the bigger the charge, the more potential for even greater conflict. This continues until the charge can no longer be contained and it "spills over" and manifests.

When this hidden charge comes out into the open because we have not been aware of the cause of the manifesting conflict, we resort to blame. We try and control the situation, all the while externalizing the cause of our discomfort. Trying to fix the problem as though the cause were something outside of ourselves actually takes us further from the possibility of achieving inner balance. Recognizing the part our shadow has played in the manifestation of distress may well be the most powerful—and often most difficult—step to take toward resolving imbalance.

As we start to look within, we see the part the shadow has played in creating the reality that is manifesting. By changing our relationship to the shadow, we will eventually discover that we can take the charge out of the situation. When the charge no longer exists within us, we will find the peace that we were originally looking for.

Because we are so lost in the unfolding drama, even imagining that internal and external balance can be restored by embracing our shadow is hard—if not downright impossible—to understand. And the fact that everyone around us is lost in a similar drama makes it even more difficult to comprehend. If there is a problem, the consensus opinion is that it is being caused by someone else, and the only way to deal with it is to "fix" it. So every model we have supports the belief that the problem is outside of us and can only be fixed by doing something about it.

It's hardly surprising that we all follow this path. The voices that offer alternatives are few and often drowned out by the collective mentality. Afraid to be different, afraid to find out their personal truths for themselves, the majority seeks safety in the consensus reality. This is often not even a conscious act.

With little in the way of support for problem solving from a different perspective, we stumble along, living the same way as we have for generations. That this way is not entirely satisfactory should be pretty obvious to us all, but as there are no alternatives on offer, what choice do we have?

Is there any other way available to us? If we were handed a model based on unconditional love that was effective, powerful, and created win-win solutions, would we welcome it with open arms? Or would we pick it apart, find faults, possibly move a little out of collective expectations, but then hurry back into the fold, into our personal little hidey hole of familiarity when questioned or challenged? We seem to be most reluctant of being seen as different from everyone around us. Our education, formal and otherwise has been pretty effective in failing to nurture compassion and tolerance.

As I travel the world, I see many societies in which various, clearly defined stereotypical patterns exist. They are like little clubs, and, if you are born into the club, you are expected to play by its long-established rules. Strangers living in areas dominated by these "clubs" may be excluded from many social activities because they are new, have different beliefs, a different skin color, or they wear different clothes. When people are shut out of their community, a likely response is to form a "club" of their own. This can either add more color and diversity to the community, or it can create conflict. Certainly, the more extreme members of any established club can feel threatened by the new club, and then the conflict is made manifest. This happens in all levels of society. Those parts of any society that feel threatened or believe themselves to be disenfranchised externalize the cause of their insecurity and look for someone, some club, some country to blame.

The entrenched patterns of failing to acknowledge the shadow and seeing the challenges we face as being caused by someone else has been going on for a very long time. The result of this belief is that the shadow has been given so much power that it has become "real." The only way to deal with "real" manifestations of the shadow is to bring even more shadow to bear, to try and moderate, manipulate, overpower, or destroy the believed cause of the conflict. People who are lost in the shadow—no matter who they are—can only seek to fix or control the manifested imbalance by building bigger walls, spending more money, employing more diplomacy, passing more legislation, using more force. There are no other ways out for those at the mercy of the shadow.

For those beginning to acknowledge the shadow and to see through their own personal experience just how powerful and important the shadow has been in creating their reality, both internal and external, the "big" issues in the world today seem insurmountable. To expect to be able to change the world of manifesting imbalance using this approach, when it appears so huge, would seem to be beyond any one person's ability. It is much easier, though, to start applying this understanding to our more immediate environment, to our family and friends. We can see immediate results and our family and friends get the benefit.

It often happens that people we are really close to challenge us the most. If the person who annoyed us intensely was someone we met socially, we would just stop seeing them—no problem. We can't just stop seeing our mother or other close relatives. It is not that simple. Often parents and children share similar information, some of which is stored in their backpacks, and they have a shared history, experiences, and genetics. Whether we are aware of it or not, it is the shared shadow that causes tension, and it is hard to understand and do anything about it. It does get easier as we realize what is happening and accept some responsibility for it, but someone has to take the first step toward reconciliation, or old patterns will just continue. Lovers and spouses are attracted to each other for many reasons, one of which is the unloved, hidden shadow. Compatibility means people are comfortable and happy with one another. It can often mean they have similar shadow issues as well. Once the honeymoon is over, it is often the shadow that presents, and the shadow will always be a major challenge in any relationship.

It is interesting to take a fresh look at what happens when a person experiences discomfort in the presence of another. We can draw upon the analogy of the tuning forks here. Without awareness, we carry charge in the backpack relating to aspects of the self we are not comfortable with— emotions and feelings that shame us, frighten us, overpower us and memories that we find challenging. These memories and feelings can be likened to a minefield. As long as we tread carefully and avoid them, they won't explode in our face. Unfortunately, we wander in the minefield blindfolded, not always knowing what is going to trigger the charges. Sometimes it is obvious. For example, often with family members, we know that mines will explode. Or that is, at least, our perception. And, of course, the other person has a similar perception and the reciprocal blame game begins again.

As explained earlier, the information we hold in our body—our emotions, our thoughts, our backpack—can all be seen as being stored as unique frequencies, and many things can trigger a reaction to these frequencies.

But it is not just our bodies that hold frequencies. The magnetic field of the earth has a wide range of frequencies as well, anyone of which can be a trigger. That is one of the reasons why you may feel different, more or less comfortable in certain environments. The frequency or information held in an environment may explain why you get a headache, feel nauseous, fidget, fall asleep quickly, or feel anxiety (for example, in the immigration hall). If you are not aware that you are simply reacting to energies or frequencies in the environment, your tendency is to blame lunch or another person—something, anything. We just do not consider that we are in such a strong symbiotic relationship to the planet we live on and that we are both receivers and transmitters of that energy.

And what do you do when you feel that headache coming on? You say, "oh no, now I have a headache," affirming that it is yours. That affirmation creates a neural connection, which will manufacture amino acids associated with a headache, and, presto, you have a headache.

Most of us are unaware of this process, and it happens so quickly that there is no time to stop it. No moment where you can say, hold on a moment, this headache is not mine, why am I taking it so personally. It is not always so simple, of course, and many times, the stress we carry will manifest as a headache, for example. All we need to do here is go back a step or two and recognize that the stress, which apparently caused the headache, was not yours either. But we have no guidelines, lost as we are in the manifesting symptoms.

In fact, the neural network is already established because of our conditioning, so it is just waiting like the minefield for someone to trigger the reaction. It is so easy for us to become and remain creatures of habit, without any conscious intention to do so. With just a little awareness, we can begin to change our manifesting reality for the better.

Two weeks after a workshop in Europe, I received an e-mail from one of the participants. She said that she awoke one morning with a headache, but when she remembered it wasn't hers, it went off looking for someone else. No more headache. So simple when you know how. But you have to catch it quickly because if you give the headache too much energy, it will be yours soon enough. You may experience headaches or other distress on a frequent basis and cannot imagine that they are not yours. This identification with such phenomena is a habit, and as long as we continue to identify with the manifesting phenomena, we are supporting the habit.

The patterning, or neural connections are so strong in us that we need to start with little things and build up, essentially slowing down the time between the stimuli and the neural link and giving us time to "change our mind."

If an external frequency matches one we hold and have charge around, then it will trigger one of the land mines, releasing a flood of neuropeptides in the body and immediately creating a physiological reaction that is beyond our control. This makes us a victim to the information stored in the backpack, with little or no awareness of what is happening to us and even less control.

Imagine that everyone is radiating out information like a mobile radio station. We may like to think that we are radiating peace and love, but reality is often quite different. We are a complex mix of transmissions, combining the many aspects of ourselves—both those that we have embraced fully and those hidden in the backpack. With or without our knowledge, we are telling the world what is in our backpack. Fortunately, not many people pick up on the transmission. But those who do invariably take the information personally, they think that the feelings or thoughts are theirs, and around they go....

But when two people are in a close relationship, they both often have the same charge in their backpacks. When they tune into each other and think about the other or come into close proximity, they trigger each other like tuning forks, and both have a familiar and uncomfortable reaction. Assuming that both continue to identify with the feelings that have been stimulated by their coming together and continue to see them as negative, uncomfortable, or even threatening, then the neural connection just keeps pumping out more amino acids associated with the feeling, which then becomes very powerful indeed. As each goes into the old conditioning of blame, they are actually increasing the charge between the two of them—whether they are conscious of this or not.

Exercise

Imagine that you are indeed eternal. Imagine that you will be born again. Not you, of course, in your present body, but the memory of who you think you are now.

Would you do anything differently knowing that you will have to come back one day and face the music? Would you be more thoughtful or less? More considerate or less?

Remember, the feelings aren't yours until you lay claim to them. The past is the past and should not control your future in any conscious or subconscious way.

Chapter Eight
The Heart of the Matter

So far we have looked at the role the brain plays in creating and supporting a reality or perhaps a "worldview" that we are currently experiencing as real. We have seen how, by association, neural connections are made and maintained, constantly reacting to various stimuli, remaking our worldview on a moment-by-moment basis to conform with our established beliefs. There is another part of our physical body that exerts control over our total system, one that may be more instrumental in creating our reactions and responses to the information we encounter on this journey. And this is the heart.

Following the fertilization of the egg, an embryonic disk forms and three layers of cells develop. One is the beginning of the sense organs and nervous system, the second is the start of the circulatory, skeletal, and muscular systems, and the third will develop into the digestive and some of the glandular systems. The heart tube forms and begins to pulsate and forces blood to circulate through blood vessels in the embryonic disk. So you had a heart before you had a brain, or, really, any other part of your body. There were the early cells that would develop into the human body over time, but right there at the very beginning was that heartbeat.

If you clap your hands, you hear one sound. This is similar to the beat of the heart; you perceive one sound, the beat. But if you look closely at the frequency components of that sound, you will see something similar to a complex chord structure some call the harmonic. This harmonic changes with each beat. This is the music that the heart is playing to each and every cell in the body. This often is random, but sometimes it falls into a coherent pattern. This energy/information/communication is transmitted to every cell and beyond.

The heart is actually singing to every cell in the body, which we detect as sound waves. As we can hear for ourselves, the sound of the thump of the heartbeat carries outside of the body, an energetic transmission from the core of our being.

The following is an excerpt from an article entitled "What Is Heart Intelligence" by James Barrett, originally written in February 2001.

New research has discovered an independent wisdom inherent to the heart that is not governed by other systems of the body. The heart has neural cells similar to those found in the brain pointing to an innate logic to the heart. The heart is autogenic, which means that it does not require a signal from the brain to beat. The impulse to contract originates in the heart muscle itself in a small bit of specialized tissue called the sinoauricular node, embedded in the wall of the right auricle. This is not dependent on ANY external stimulus, and no

*other part of the body controls this function.
You can be brain dead and your heart can still
maintain the cells. When the heart stops beating
the body begins to crumble.*

*In the past it was thought that the brain
was the central organizer for the body. Today, we
know that the heart is the key rhythm regulator.
The heart receives and translates information
from the other physical systems as well as from a
non-local component, and broadcasts info-energy
back to every cell including the DNA matrix. The
heart's primary job is to maintain balance in the
body. It does this with every beat, 60 to 100 times
per minute on average. Within each beat is a
symphony of frequencies that trigger responses
from the other systems. The result is what you
experience physically and emotionally.*

*Heart Intelligence is at the core of many
recent books by some of the most prestigious
doctors and researchers in the medical
community. The heart's amazing properties
and influences over other bodily systems places
it properly at the core of health research and
makes the inevitable connection between
science and spirituality. Heart Intelligence is a
phrase used to describe numerous attributes
of the electrical and magnetic energy waves
radiating from the heart that influence
functions and systems, including the brain.
When the waves of these energy fields are "Phi
coherent" or in phase with Phi relationships,*

specific beneficial results occur within the mind and body.

The heart through these biological communication systems, has a significant influence on the function of our brains and all our bodily systems.

The electromagnetic fields of the beating heart generate pressure waves, which in turn generates neurotransmitters thus creating other proteins and hormones. The inter play of energies at a cellular level send nerve impulses and corresponding chemicals (proteins) in a cascade throughout the body. The charge felt is Energy in motion, E-motion.

I have come to believe, like the early Sufic text states, that "the Heart is the seat of God when opened, but a tomb when closed."

An open heart is one that has the ability to play a large variability of frequencies. It can be thought of poetically as flexibility or an openness of the heart to receive and play other music. When the Heart gets stuck or closed in an even metronome of beats the music gets fixed and the ability of the body to respond is greatly diminished. Communication takes an open heart in order to receive that which is being shared. The Study of this in medical research is under the guise of heart rate variability (HRV). This is known to be the single common thread between all illness, social disorders and cellular aging.

According to this information, the brain is not responsible for the manufacture of the proteins, it is simply following the heart's directions. The heart has its own intelligence. What then dictates to the heart which information, which songs, it will sing to the cells and the outside world? It has to be based upon a combination of genetics, soul memory, personal experience, and the accumulated shadow. A happy, open heart will be able to dance with or sing along to any tune in its environment,while a closed heart loses some of this ability. Assuming that the heart has neural cells, could it be possible that the heart has a brain-like capacity?

The article by James Barrett indicates that the heart has an innate logic of its own. If this is the case, it would mean that certain "external" frequencies of information trigger the firing of these neural cells within the heart, which then play a part in the manufacturing of neuropeptides. It then follows that the heart, like the brain, could have developed unique ways of responding / reacting to various frequencies.

These unique ways become habits, which may well be unconscious reactions to external stimuli. Thus they seem to be outside of our control and end up reinforcing any shadow aspects of the self.

Although I have spent a great deal of time and energy talking about the shadow, I do not want it to sound as though I am obsessed with this aspect of our make-up. However, I do think it important to recognize just how much we are unaware of and to what degree it controls us. It would surely benefit us to uncover as much of this as possible and bring it into our conscious awareness.

I believe that our body remembers everything that ever happened to it—every thought, every emotion. Nothing is lost, nothing is forgotten. We may have difficulty accessing some of those memories but that does not mean they are not there.

When we experience trauma, depending upon our ability to deal with it at the time it occurs, we will either embrace it and move on, meaning that we have coped, at least on the surface, or we will try and shut it out. We cannot simply erase a memory, but we can deny it ever happened. This would appear to be a self-protective mechanism designed to prevent us from revisiting the trauma emotionally, psychologically, or physiologically.

Being the center of our universe and quite possibly the major control center, the heart remembers the experience that we perceived as traumatic. It remembers the feeling or the frequencies associated with the trauma and attempts to avoid those frequencies by the physical process of denial.

The heart begins to close down. Obviously it cannot really close down, as we would die if it did, but it does seem to have a defence mechanism whereby it walls off or limits its ability to be in open communication with its total environment when the information contained in that environment is perceived to be a threat to the self. This is a learned behavior. It is unlikely the tiny baby will have such a defence mechanism when it is born, and it acquires this through personal experience. This closing down of the heart is the heart's inability to feel and be in relationship with all of the information it is receiving/picking up from all around it.

The heart may be so successful in this process that we never consciously revisit traumatic events. Trauma may surface in the dream state, when the mind is no longer so alert and having to deal with day-to-day situations or is lost in trivia. Trauma may resurface when we are tired or stressed, but for most of us, the heart/brain connection is doing its job of shielding us from those memories we perceive as traumatic.

It is where those memories are very intense and have a strong charge that they keep popping into our awareness, even though we maybe denying the memories. We can never wipe the memory out. It is always there, and only the process of denial has pushed the memory beneath the surface where it has become a part of the subconsciousness that still exerts so much control over us.

There is a strong possibility that, even though a memory of a trauma is buried in our subconscious, that memory is still playing a part in creating our view of the world. This reinforces the memory because not only can we not effectively deny it, but it is being recreated in our world on a daily basis.

The degree to which these memories manifest in our lives depends, I think, upon the intensity of the charge held in the subconscious or shadow part of ourselves. A weak charge causes little or no manifestation, and strong charge results in obvious manifestation. The difficulty we have is in recognizing the source of the manifesting energies because the memory that is helping to create our worldview has been buried so long. Out of sight, out of mind.

It is interesting to make the connection between information as a collection of various frequencies, the beat of the heart, and the neural cells in the brain and the heart. As discussed earlier, given repeated, habitual identification with certain frequencies, the neural network in the heart/brain will form connections. Over time, these connections can get locked in, and any time the body picks up the frequency of the remembered stressor, it will immediately go into a pre-determined reaction, creating a feeling of discomfort. The heart seems to play an important part in how the brain makes connections.

When our environment is trying to remind us of our past, sometimes gently, sometimes not so gently, it may well be reinforcing particular neural connections. Again, this process is believed to be outside of our control. This then has the effect of making us victims to memories. No matter how much we would like to move on from the past, as long as there is any identification with trauma held in the body, we will continue to project that out into the world. And the world we find ourselves in will continue to trigger old, long-denied memories.

When two people who hold something in common within their shadows come together, this triggers one of those land mines in each of them, and the old memory of some perceived hurt arises and takes control. This is so well established that they are both powerless to change this reaction. Each will then go further into denial to try and deal with the pain of the situation. This, in turn, causes the hearts to attempt to close down even further, to shut out the memory, but it is too late. The heart/brain have already made the connections, and the chemicals are, once again, flooding the body. Since there was no physical cause for the reaction, presumably it was an emotional response. What I am trying to explore here is why there is such a strong reaction and what can be done about it.

I was once at a small gathering of friends, and all was going well until someone in the room mentioned one of the young men's absent girlfriend. This young man had a quiet, shy nature and was obviously embarrassed to have the subject of his girlfriend brought up in company. Very quickly, he went from being happy and relaxed through a whole range of emotions. He became agitated, uncomfortable, his skin flushed red, he became quite defensive, and ultimately aggressive as old neural networks fired off a memory of his relationship with the woman. Gradually, he was able to "get control" of himself again, in essence, let go of the feeling and stop the manufacture of the chemicals causing his discomfort.

We mentioned our "comfort zone" earlier, as representing a place of inner peace and contentment. Remember, when we say we are out of our comfort zone, it means we are experiencing a situation that is either externally threatening, or we are having to face some shadow aspect of ourselves. This young man was certainly out of his comfort zone. A memory had been triggered, one of those land mines exploded, and he went into automatic reaction, where he temporarily had no control over the way he reacted to the mention of his girlfriend. An example of being a victim to the shadow. This was a strong reaction, and one that was noticeable to everyone on the room, but often our reactions are less obvious. We react when we are reminded of our shadow, which, of course, is included in the great area of our subconscious.

We are either reacting or responding to information all of the time, but when we are self-absorbed, we do not notice any change in our mental, emotional, or physical state. The information that we are picking up is being read by the heart—or not—depending upon the availability of the heart to receive the communication. When the heart is "open," which implies it is not being reminded of any shadow aspects, it is embracing all the information it receives, not judging, not being afraid, not running away, but simply being with whatever arises. This is influenced by many factors, of course, and is therefore relative.

We can deny the existence of the shadow all of our lives, deny feeling uncomfortable, deny feeling threatened. If we have mastered the art of denial, nothing seems to get through or trouble us. We may think we have control of our feelings and that is a good thing, but where feelings are denied, we are physically, mentally, and emotionally at risk. When the heart is closed down, it has lost some of its ability to be available. Simply put, the shadow or the denied part of the self is taking control, without the individual's awareness (of course).

When the heart cannot feel or accept the information energetically without going into a negative reaction, the only way it can feel safe is to try and manipulate the external environment so that it does not have to feel the information anymore. If the individual must modify the reality they find themselves in to feel safe, chances are that someone will suffer as a result—the person or persons whom the individual is blaming for their discomfort. This is hardly a win-win situation. The real cause of the individual's discomfort is a closed heart and, as long as the person seeks answers externally, the heart will never learn to be open.

It would appear that as long as we seek answers outside of the self, not only will our hearts never learn to be open, trusting, and loving, but they will close down even more. When the heart closes down, it loses its flexibility and becomes a fearful heart. A fearful heart not only transmits

its fear to the rest of the cells in the body, causing chemicals of a destructive nature to fill the body, it sends this message out to the world. By the simple nature of cause and effect— attracting that which we are—the fearful heart finds itself in ever more fearful situations and is under constant pressure to correct the situation. It tries to do this by exerting ever more control over its surroundings and those it blames for its own insecurity.

We had a couple at a three-day workshop, which was being held in the wife's home town. When these two had married, they had moved away to set up their own home, and, as a result, Ann (not her real name) spent less time with her mother than she had in the past. On the second day, Ann told me that she had to visit her mother that evening and that she was not looking forward to it. Her relationship with her mother had been pretty uncomfortable for a long time, and she was nervously expecting more of the same.

When she came back into the workshop on the next morning, after spending an evening with her mother, she came into the room with a great smile and radiating peacefulness. She shared her story with the other workshop participants, telling them how her relationship with her mother had been poor up to now. Then she described her visit with her mother and how she had spent one and a half hours with her the previous evening. That had been a record, she said, and it had been their best visit ever—so comfortable that she could have spent another hour and a half there, something unheard of in the past. Her husband confirmed this, saying how he had sat through the hour and a half open-mouthed in disbelief.

What had happened? What was different? The only thing Ann could think of was that she had applied the teachings of the first two days to her meeting with her mother and the change had been remarkable in both of them.

Here, as in any difficult relationship, we simply have two people who have a shared memory of pain and suffering coming together. The people do not have to be related—it could be someone at work or another casual acquaintance.

Anytime we connect and communicate with another, the possibility is there that we have something in common, something that is hidden away in our backpacks. And when common shadow issues exist, each person triggers the other and brings the shadow to the surface. Each goes into denial and blames the other, which only exacerbates the situation. The more we blame or externalize the apparent cause of our discomfort, the more we identify with the feeling of helplessness, the more chemicals associated with that discomfort the body produces. And so we get caught in a pretty vicious cycle that, if pursued, leads to even more discomfort. This process continues to take us even further out of any comfort zone we may have believed we had, tension builds and builds between the two people, often leading to open conflict or hostility.

Here were have a mother and her daughter, both experiencing the same pain, each blaming the other—a situation many of us find ourselves in. Or at least we would, if we noticed what was going on instead of losing ourselves in reaction. When we spoke about how and why we develop such conditioned behavioral patterns and what we can do to change those patterns in the workshop, it must have reminded Ann of her relationship with her mother. And she realized that if the situation with her mother was to change and improve, she had to take the first step.

Once we imagine ourselves to be lost in any relationship full of conflict, the current or accepted way to "deal" with it becomes a challenge in itself. It requires us to face and move beyond the conditioning that seems to have created the state of conflict in the first place. If we had been able to face and move beyond old conditioning, it is likely we would never have found ourselves in such an uncomfortable place at all.

When the shadow arises, we are—to some degree—powerless. Had we been able to deal with the shadow in a loving way, there would be no shadow. But having given the shadow so much energy in the past, it becomes a very powerful force in your life and plays a major part in what you experience and how you deal with whatever presents itself to you. So life can appear really complicated. You have this unloved shadow part of yourself, which you keep denying, yet still it continues to present.

The manifestation of the shadow often creates tension in relationships, whether with yourself or another. You try and deal with not only your own denied shadow, but the denied shadow of the other as well—assuming you are trying for resolution and not just getting lost in the chemical haze produced by the body as it loses control.

Ann had previously gotten lost in the haze, as had her mother. It is hardly surprising that they limited their time together—until the fateful meeting on that Saturday evening, after the daughter had attended two days of workshop, where we had spoken about the heart and how it closes down or goes into a negative reaction when it feels threatened and some of the reasons why this is so. This way of dealing with information sets us up to experience involuntary reactions to certain information that we had previously judged as negative. No wonder we try and avoid dealing with the shadow, a process that to many must feel very disagreeable.

If our reality has, in any way, been created by our shadow, then asking a person to try and restore harmony to that reality without embracing their "dark side" cannot be successful. Until we see the cause of our discontent, we will continue to blame and externalize, perpetuating and aggravating the situation. Similarly, asking a person to resolve conflicting situations in their life by embracing their dark side is quite likely doomed to failure as well. Because of the nature of denial, it is very challenging to have to see the part we have played in creating the conflict we experience. If every man is indeed the author of their own misfortunes, then we have indeed dug a deep hole for ourselves, and the way out is not to continue digging. But try telling that to someone in a hole. We just do not want to hear about the part we are playing because this brings up the specter of opening a Pandora's box that is just too overwhelming.

But opening this box does not have to be overwhelming. If we take this process step by step, move slowly into a different way of looking at ourselves and our relationship with the external, it can be easy, safe, and even fun. If we take the disagreeable aspect of embracing our shadow too seriously, we will never start the process. To begin with, we need to redefine our relationship with ourselves. We can start taking some of the pressure off the information stored in the backpack by not taking ourselves too seriously—easy to say, but very difficult to do. We should not approach this process head on, as it is way too difficult. To, all of a sudden, discard everything you have taken seriously in the past is not going to happen. So remember, small steps.

Start with a gentle feeling, not an intense one that is likely to take control of you the moment it pops into your awareness, but something inconsequential. In the training, it helps if you can focus on another person and read something of the information they are transmitting. It is easy to do this, and, in fact, we are doing it all of the time. Most of us, most of the time, are not aware we are doing this. When we do notice a thought or a feeling, conditioning dictates that we think it is ours! Lost again.

In order to notice what is going on around us, in an objective way, we need to be aware of what we are feeling at any given moment. This could be the hardest part of the training. Sitting quietly, notice your breathing, relax, try not to feel anything. I have found over the years that the harder people try to feel something, the less likely they are to succeed. Just be still and notice whatever thoughts or emotions pop into your mind. This process of information arising in your awareness is going on all the time, but normally we are so busy that we don't notice it.

When you get the hang of just sitting quietly and noticing, try recalling a memory of a really happy time. You may be hopeless at visualizing, but no matter. You don't need a full-length movie, but just a momentary feeling.

Did you notice a change in your thoughts or feelings? The intensity of the thought or feeling is not important, and don't dismiss any thought or feeling as "just" your imagination. With practice this gets much easier and more obvious. It is happening to me as I sit here at my computer. I stopped writing for a moment and began thinking of someone close to me and noticed quite a strong change in how my body felt. When we concentrate on another person and notice a change in how we are feeling, physically or emotionally, we may as force of habit, have thought that the feeling belonged to us.

The feeling you experience may be quite strong, and one that you recognize as being "yours." Simply because the thought or feeling is familiar, something you have identified with in the past, does not mean that it is—or ever has been—yours. You are simply reacting to a memory. The transmission from the other person can trigger something you hold in your backpack, which may or may not result in your having an emotional or physiological reaction. It is often the case that you are not triggered by the transmission you pick up on because you have no charge around that particular frequency. Just notice the change in the feeling and say to yourself, "This is not my feeling, it is just how my body is interpreting the information from so and so."

Unless you have consciously or unconsciously identified with the feeling too strongly—which would have created a significant cascade of chemicals through your body—you should notice that the feeling or thought passes out of your awareness as easily as it came in.

Naturally we find it easier to let go of information that does not trigger a strong reaction in our system. The stronger the charge we hold around certain information or certain frequencies, the more likely we are to go into a significant reaction. The stronger the reaction, the less control we have over the situation that develops, and the less control we have, the more powerless we feel, and the more we try and control the situation. This all leads to a deepening of the hole and greater difficulty in finding a way out. It also prevents us from responding in the most suitable way to situations that arise or present in our life.

When we can associate thoughts and feelings that we experience with either transmissions from another person or with environmental energies, it takes the pressure off us. It allows us to feel the information more fully without going into a conditioned identification with the thought or feeling, which happens because previously we may have identified with and personalized painful feelings, kept them as ours, and suffered their effects.

Now, by recognizing that the feelings are not ours, but just feelings, we are saying to our heart, "It's okay, I can feel this, and it will not hurt me because it isn't mine. I don't have to carry this feeling into my future any longer." By practicing this now and then throughout the day, we gradually learn to separate that which we believed to be our thoughts and feelings from what we are picking up from others or from the environment. We have begun the process of re-opening the heart.

If we realize that a feeling, whether physical or emotional, is not ours, but rather that it is just how our body is reacting to information it is picking up from its environment, it's easier for us to stop judging the feeling as good or bad. In workshops, we have witnessed many times how the body physically reacts to certain information—be it environmental or from another person. Learning to know when this is happening and stepping in and changing the "channel" before the process completes its cycle of creating the physical reality of that feeling is an important step to greater personal freedom. As you might imagine, if many of the physical symptoms you experience are not yours, but rather how your body reacts to external stimuli, there is a lot happening to you that is unnecessary. If you were to have the means whereby you could determine and act upon what is and isn't yours before the feelings took hold and manifested more solidly in the body, there is no telling just how much physical discomfort you could avoid.

As we continue to personalize and identify with many, if not all, of the thoughts and feelings that pop into our awareness throughout the day, we will judge those feelings as good or bad out of habit. We are not talking about moral judgments now. If there were no shadow, there could be no conflicting patterns within us, and therefore nothing to judge outside of us. This judgment that we are referring to is that inner voice that perceives itself to be better or worse than others.

Whilst we continue to judge, we maintain a polarized state of being, always in conflict with others and our environment. This state of conflict is simply another manifestation of the shadow, showing us aspects of ourselves that we have yet to embrace and love. We often find ourselves in a catch-22 situation, believing ourselves to be separate, isolated beings—always us and them. Yet, as attachment to personality falls away, we come to understand how inter-connected we are with others and our environment. But what steps can we take that will lead out of this cycle of beliefs? My feeling is that by noticing any change in how we feel when we think of another person, we begin to see that much of the information we have associated with in the past, truly believing it to be ours, has, in fact, nothing to do with us personally at all.

By noticing our reactions to the energetic transmissions of others, we begin to see that we are not quite as isolated as we thought. If we are picking up information from others and our environment, then there must be some force, some intelligence, that is connecting us. When we see that much of who we thought we were is simply how we react to information received, then it follows that those around us are being affected by our transmissions as well and are not just who they have thought themselves to be in the past either.

One of the major benefits of practicing opening up and feeling, and the consequent knowing that the feeling is not yours, is that you can stop judging the feeling as good or bad and simply refer to it as a feeling. It is so much easier to feel a broader range of information without judging it if you know that the feeling is not actually yours. Continuing though life in the old, conditioned way, of associating with or personalizing every thought or feeling that enters your awareness cannot give you any lasting sense of peace. Because of how the memories are held or identified with in the heart, we would have to continue to judge the information as good or bad. We would remain locked into sorting the feelings into two piles—those that are acceptable to you and those that aren't. Whilst we seek happiness by running from the shadow, that happiness can never materialize because the shadow is still responsible, in part, for creating the reality that you keep manifesting.

Exercise

Have you ever felt as though your heart was wanting to burst open—with joy, with sadness? Not the heart attack feeling, but the pericardium itself wanting to expand?

In our experience, this could indicate that your heart is being asked to embrace frequencies or information that previously you may have denied or judged as bad. If the heart has its own innate intelligence, then it follows that it may also have a memory. Obviously, if you are having a heart attack, then seek help immediately, but if it is just the heart wanting to open, what should you do?

Listen to your heart taking a new step.

Chapter Nine
Embracing the Shadow

In his work *Mind and Matter*, Erwin Schrödinger said, "Every man's world picture is and always remains a construct of his mind and cannot be proved to have any other existence." It is not the world that we are creating but just our view of it. However, our worldview is conditioned by the collective, and it is the collective who is creating the manifesting reality.

There seem to be a heck of a lot of people in the world today who desire world peace, yet we are nowhere near that dream, and haven't been for millennia—if ever. Why, if so many people desire peace, do we not have it? The shadow comes to mind as being one of the leading culprits.

I have seen it written that greed, fear, and ignorance are the veils that prevent us from knowing our true nature. Ignorance, the forgetfulness at the moment of birth; greed, the desire to make the personality as happy and safe as possible at whatever cost; and fear, the fear of the unknown that keeps us a prisoner to the commonly held beliefs of our time.

For us to manifest a peaceful world, we must first find that peace within us. Whilst we are locked into judging everyone and everything around us, a product of our own internal unrest, we maintain this state of inner conflict, which then manifests outside of ourselves. No wonder there is so little peace on earth. It is hard to avoid feelings that undermine our very nature, to not come from a place of always needing to be right. We exist at the center of our universe, and there is a part in each of us that says our way is the best way, the right way, especially when others are "different" from us.

The externalization of the shadow has so strongly manifested and become such a powerful, dominant reality—or, more correctly, a worldview held by the majority—that it truly appears that the only way to deal with it, is to do more to control it. Which of course just keeps creating more of the same. This process is not unlike a hot air balloon soaring through the sky. If you stop putting hot air into the balloon, it is going to fall out of the sky, and no one wants to be the first to stop feeding a reality, for fear of what might happen. It is unlikely that all of the energy can be taken from the collective worldview all at once, this would be extremely traumatic and inadvisable, but rather let the hot air out little by little, and see what happens.

Our continued association with the feelings arising in our awareness could be our personal hot air. When we can say to ourselves, "This is just a thought, this is just a feeling, I don't have to get lost in it because it isn't mine," the process of deflating the balloon begins. And because the feelings aren't mine, I won't have to carry them around forever in my backpack so that they are around to constantly plague me in the future. If I don't have to take this feeling seriously, then I don't have to judge it. It is simply a feeling, one of many, but just a feeling. The feeling of, say, anxiety. Hmm, not a pleasant feeling if I were to take it seriously, but, if I stop identifying with anxiety, then I am giving myself permission to feel it without getting lost in it. This is, I believe, important. To be willing and able to feel everything without ever getting lost.

I think one of the main reasons why many of us have avoided opening up to feelings in the past is because we have so very few role models that teach us otherwise. We may have had no practice, certainly not when young, of freely expressing ourselves. There are many reasons why we may grow up without ever being able to express our emotions. Many children, particularly boys, are not given permission to show their emotions. We may be afraid of being overpowered by those emotions, disabled by their intensity, or frightened by the pain of a memory. It may be a fear of being seen as weak or out of control. A mind lost in the effects of the shadow can come up with all sorts of reasons to continue denying what the body / heart is feeling.

When the heart reacts to information that it has repeatedly identified with, the neurons fire off in those predictable patterns from the past, flooding the body with the same chemicals, and physiologically creating the same inner reality. Lost again. We have talked a lot about conditioned reaction, and how, in the past, we have established particular neural connections, but we may find ourselves facing a new experience—one that does not have its own unique, pre-determined reaction. Our response/ reaction to this new experience is still going to be the product of our past. Even though we might not have this particular memory, we can still only work with what we have. And we should not forget the power contained in the subconscious.

As the heart responds to various external stimuli and sings its song to all the cells in the body, the body sends out waves of information, related to the heartbeat and, later on, associated with the chemicals created as a result of our interaction with our environment. This transmission then influences our surroundings and attracts situations into our lives that support the way we are feeling. We are totally lost now because our environment and the people in it are all confirming how we are feeling, thus justifying our having had or identified with those feelings in the first place. Hardly any wonder that not many people try and break out of that patterning—it is enough to drive anybody crazy.

Slowly, by practice, we begin to realize that we are not our thoughts, nor are we our feelings. We are not even the experience. We are the one having the experience. So many times in the past, we have taken the experience personally and by doing so have become the experience. This can only lead to more confusion as, by losing ourself in the experience just creates yet another experience, and, already lost, we just go deeper into a particular worldview that has no basis whatsoever in any fact.

By developing non-judgment, which is a product of realizing that the thoughts or feelings that arise in your awareness have nothing to do with you at all, you are, in fact, learning to open your heart. Training the heart to be open and fearless has so many benefits on so many levels that it should be something we all work at a little each day. Even if we take a purely personal point of view, knowing that our hearts are singing to every cell in our being, it does not take much of an imagination to realize that if our hearts are singing happy, healthy songs, then our physical bodies will benefit. If we are singing angry, fearful songs, then our bodies will suffer.

Ann, whom I talked about a few pages ago, took the words to heart when she visited her mother that Saturday evening. Even though they were still transmitting both the loved and the shadow aspects of their natures, the young woman recognized what was happening. She now knew that both she and her mother were feeling the same pain, the same sense of disconnection. So, instead of reacting as she had done previously, she remained in the situation with an open heart. And this open heart was refusing to identify with or react to the chemicals that her body produced when she was in her mother's presence. She told us that she repeated over and over to herself, "This is just a feeling, it is not mine." Very soon the body stopped producing the chemicals that were creating a physical response to the situation, which she had previously seen as personal, negative, and something to be avoided.

As she practiced allowing the feeling but not identifying with it, Ann was learning to love her own shadow. When she avoided going into the old, conditioned reaction, it created a heart space of safety that her mother could literally fall into without her own issues being triggered. Conflict could arise only when both maintained a closed heart. When the daughter began to stop identifying with the feelings knowing they were not hers, but just feelings or memories from the past, she was opening her heart to receive the heart transmission from her mother without judging it. When the mother's transmission was met with love, not judgment, it failed to provoke the old reaction that the mother was conditioned to expect. So instead of the tension developing, harmony grew between the two, and the wound that had troubled these two women for so long was at last healed.

It was as easy and simple as that. It did not require either of them to try and work out the problems from within the reality that had created the problems they had been experiencing. All it took was one of the people involved to practice compassion, the desire to help the other, to no longer take that which arose personally.

You might be thinking that by not identifying with the feeling, you are simply going back into old patterns of denial or creating new ones, but this is not the case. Denial closes down the heart and blocks out memories because of the feelings we associate with those memories. A closed heart cannot feel and, when the heart cannot feel, it gives the intellect permission to create an artificial safety at the expense of others and the environment. There we go again, imposing our insecurity on the world around us.

When we stop identifying with feelings, we are really allowing those feelings to be present in the body. So rather than denying these feelings, which would shut them out, we are actively opening up to more and more feelings. We get to experience a much broader range of feelings because we no longer take them so seriously.

I believe it is unrealistic to expect a person, who has spent their life not getting in touch with their feelings to all of a sudden open up to feeling everything. And not everyone, of course, has been closed off from feeling. Many people—people who are extremely sensitive and may have trouble establishing boundaries—feel what they consider to be way too much. Each of us feels quite a lot, much more than we acknowledge. Feeling is not the issue, but it is the ability to be objective about the feeling that is not so easy. We all feel, but for the most part, we are lost in the feeling, so there is no place from which we can objectively view the situation.

As long as the range of emotions that we feel fit within the box we call "our comfort zone" we are okay, happy, and at peace with the world. It is the emotional energy lying outside of the comfort zone that we have trouble with. If you have spent a lifetime establishing a concept of who you are and have become attached—as we all do—to that concept, then anything that does not conform to your perception of right and wrong, good and bad, gets rejected, often without any conscious acknowledgement.

Considering our past, expecting that any of us could just open up to feeling everything without reservations is naive. To help overcome the obvious challenges, we need to develop a new way of seeing who we are. A way that will change our relationship to the information stored in the backpack. It is almost as though we have to learn how to feel all over again—only this time from a much more adult perspective.

We need to find a safe place from which to start this journey, to have a good, reliable map, and plenty of signposts along the way because the moment we don't feel safe, we easily revert to the old way of dealing with what is happening to us—we react, externalize, blame, and close down. The practice of opening up to a feeling that we believe to be coming from someone or something else gives us that safety. It gives us a place from which we can practice being the observer of a feeling. Knowing the feeling is a transmission from another person makes it safe for us to feel it. We can say, for example, "This is the feeling of anxiety. This is what this emotion feels like. It is not mine, but just how I am reacting/responding to someone else's feeling."

When we do this, we take a significant step toward healing our own heart. We are no longer denying feelings but have created a safe place from which to begin feeling so much more than we previously felt safe doing. Chances are that along the way we will get lost now and again. We subconsciously "tune into" someone who has similar shadow issues to our own, and this triggers off the chemical cascade. Yet as we practice opening up and telling ourselves that the feeling, whatever it may be, is not ours, we are rewiring the neural net in the brain, we are sending new messages to our hearts. We are feeling so much more without getting lost in the feeling.

In his book, *Dreaming While Awake*, Arnold Mindell, Ph.D writes about various ways of dealing with situations of tension:

> "The other possibility is that we move out of time and space and let go of our identity. We become lucid about our sentient experience and, even before it manifests positive or negative figures, we become edgeless. Even before we can talk about a tension, we change and let go of our hold on time and go with the flow. Such moments require a lot of awareness, personal courage and flexibility."

Essentially, Mindell is talking about compassion and the open heart. I am not sure I agree with his comments about how challenging this can be. Any degree of challenge is relative to the individual person practicing this way. If we come from the old model of relating and taking that which arises personally, we will certainly be challenged. If we can find a different way of relating to the information that presents to us, this practice can become effortless. Yet without the training involved in gradually opening the heart by redefining how we react or respond to life's experiences, I can agree with Mindell, that it would take a lot of awareness, personal courage, and flexibility to reach this state of edgelessness. In fact, if I had just been presented with this piece of information about stepping outside of time and space and been given no background or guidelines, I would say it would be almost impossible to do as he is suggesting.

But given what we have discovered about the heart, understanding the above statement from the heart's point of view, we can see how we might achieve this edgeless state more easily. The heart picks up on energetic transmissions and, even before we can take a breath, it has begun the process of manufacturing chemicals. Simultaneously, the heart sends a message to the brain, which adds to the chemical cascade, thereby reducing us to highly reactive beings. Seeing what is happening at least gives us a starting point.

By finding a way to increase the time between the heart receiving the information and reacting by sending signals to the brain, we create a moment of choice. Life should be a series of choices, instead it has become a continuum of reactive moments. We may perceive we have choice, but the framework from within, which we get to choose, is limited by our past.

One of the first steps to help us choose and not react is to develop the ability to notice any change in how or what we are feeling. We are all feeling emotions, thinking thoughts all of the time, but so few of us take the time to notice, to be the observer. We are so used to identifying with "our" thoughts and feelings that it is very difficult to escape our subjective nature. If we cannot know what we are feeling at any given point in time, how are we going to notice any change to that state?

It is difficult to see through the conditioning that comes with the physical body because we have lost ourselves to such a degree in the personality that we don't know the full extent of what it means to be objective about what's going on. We have set up all of the neuropathways, we have established limited areas where our heart feels safe, we have conditioned reactions to just about every situation. We go through life thinking that everything is under control until one of our buttons gets pushed, one of the land mines explodes, and we immediately go into a predetermined reaction.

By developing ways of releasing the charge of the shadow in gentle non-threatening ways, it becomes easier for us to regain some objectivity in our lives. With this objectivity comes a new awareness of how we are sustaining our view of reality, of the world around us. Internally, we are sending a new message to our heart, we are telling our heart it is safe once again to feel the emotions previously held in memory as painful. We can do this, and the heart will believe us because we have learned a new way of being in the world—one that undoes old neural connections instead of strengthening them, one that does not catapult us into painful reactions every time we pick up information that was once stored in our backpack.

Whilst we continue to identify with commonly held patterns of who we are, our external reality reflects that back to us to varying degrees. Whatever role we assume, by choice or otherwise, we will find others fitting into a similar category, and this collection of like minds can develop into a sub-culture. Many people find personal identity through association with their sub-culture, which gives them a sense of belonging, of identification. If you are a musician, you spend time with other musicians, and you would tend to associate more with people who like and play the same music as you do. Within the world of music, you define yourself by what you do. You are a musician, and you play such and such. If you are an airline pilot, chances are good that you love flying, and your world is the cockpit of an airplane. You associate with other people who like flying, this is your identity, this is who you are. We are always so much more than any limitations or associations, but the point here is that, as long as we believe ourselves to be "something," then our world reflects that something back to us and continually affirms that is who we are. We tend to subconsciously create a very safe environment. So our beliefs and perceptions, our language, our skin color, our religion, our nationality, the football or baseball team that we support, all play a part in creating the reality that we identify with and often take very seriously indeed.

When we change or stop taking ourselves and our reality quite so seriously, our external world will also change to reflect the inner changes. Why would you want to change your reality? On a personal level, a reality that contains a

lot of pain and suffering is often enough reason to seek
change. On a more communal level, no matter who you
believe yourself to be, imagine how the complexity of who
you are is affecting everyone around you. Every moment of
every day, the love that you are, the shadow that you carry
with you affect those you love, and—just as importantly—
those you don't. If you are unhappy, if your world is an
unhappy place, it would be a good reason to change. If
you are angry, and your world is an angry place, if you are
depressed and your world is a depressed place, these are all
good reasons to change. You may be a happy, very loving
person and think there is no need to change, your world is
a happy place. Yet your world is not contained within your
sub-culture, your world includes everything in the world,
without exception.

While there is abuse of anyone or anything in the world,
your world is not quite so happy as you may have thought.
Maintaining a sense of isolation, of separation, or of identity
with your sub-culture cannot change the fact that you are a
part of the world. You are affected by that world, and you
are affecting that world just by your being who you are. You
don't have to actually do anything to affect or change the
world, you simply have to continue being who you are.

To change the world you must first change yourself. In
the very process of changing the self, the world will change,
you don't have to be out there doing all the time. The
transmission of who you are and who you are becoming has a
powerful impact upon the world. Only by practicing this for
yourself will you see the effects your thoughts and feelings
have upon your environment, how those thoughts and
feelings are co-creating and maintaining your worldview.

We can change who we believe ourselves to be by breaking the cycle, by slowing time down to the point where we can begin to experience a thought or a feeling, catching it before it overwhelms.

The challenge is to notice when a thought or a feeling arises in your awareness, as it will, as it constantly does, and to simply observe that thought or feeling. Do not take that thought or feeling personally, do not identify with it. It is just a thought. It is just a feeling. A way to help understand and develop this practice is to imagine that each thought or feeling that enters your awareness is a helium-filled balloon. The balloon may have a label on it, identifying the particular thought or emotion it represents. The balloon may be colored, a color you associate with the particular thought or emotion that is coming into your awareness. And you sit quietly, watch as each balloon rises in your awareness. The practice is to develop the ability to observe the balloons and not to grab hold of any of them, claiming them as yours.

Whatever presents is just information arising in your awareness. It is common to believe the thoughts or emotions to be yours because, in the past, you continually identified with that thought or feeling and saw it as being yours. There will often be times when you reach out and grab a hold of one or more of the balloons, this is just conditioning, and this tendency will fade the more you practice. Affirming something over and over again, with or without awareness, will make it seem as though it is an aspect of your personality, a part of who you believe yourself to be.

It is when you grasp or personalize a thought or feeling, saying, "This is my thought, this is my feeling, this is my belief system," that you start the process of cementing those neurons into place. And, as we have previously said, this sets you up for more of the same in your future. Being born into a body with genetic and soul memory is the starting point of the journey—at least in this physical reality.

Exercise

Imagine wearing a backpack where you have put all the experiences that you did not want to deal with in the past. Imagine, the more you have filled the backpack, the heavier it has become. And the heavier it is, the more you are likely to go into a spontaneous reaction whenever someone pushes you into your unloved past.

Can you recall any moments when you have gone straight into reaction because of something someone has said or done?

Were you in control of yourself? Did you feel good during or after the reaction? Has this situation repeated itself throughout your life? Would you like to be free of this charge you hold?

Don't wait to try changing your mind when you are confronted by the old pattern or person. Because memory kicks in very quickly, that would be too late . Try and bring to mind a situation or person that continues to trouble you. As the picture gets stronger in your awareness, notice how the emotions change in your body. As you feel each wave of emotion, recognize, once again, that this is just a memory from the past, it is no longer yours, and let it go.

Practice will improve your ability to breathe through the emotional charge.

Chapter Ten
Reopening the Heart for Business

From an early age, we are conditioned to take our thoughts and feelings personally. This would seem to be a part of what it means to be human, yet it is not necessarily the complete picture. We identify with this information partly because it is human nature—or we assume it to be human nature—and partly because there is no one telling us otherwise. Just because you took a piece of information and, over time, became that information, does not mean that it is who you are. It is certainly who you have become and—logic would seem to dictate—who you will be tomorrow, but it is not who you are.

To make the journey of embracing the shadow both possible and practical, we can imagine a series of stepping stones, each taking us further from old, limiting ways of being toward a more self-empowered, compassionate place. The ease with which we make this transition depends very much on how "stuck" we are in our current perceptions. The degree to which we take ourselves and our drama so personally and seriously now is a product of our past, but it does not matter where it came from—whether genetics, soul memory, or personal experience. We may appear to have no control over our past, but the goal is not to control the past. All we need to do is simply recognize the past for what it is, our past, and as such, it should not control our future. We may certainly be guided by our past, the lessons learned and experience gained, but there is no need for us to be victims to that past.

If you haven't already done so, just for a moment, accept that we are energetic beings, in human form, each one of us sending out a complex array of signals into the world. Our individual signals are adding to and mixing with an amazing collection of other signals or transmissions coming from all of the frequencies in the electro-magnetic spectrum. I call this the cosmic soup. There are probably more scientific terms, but the words "cosmic soup" or perhaps "the sea of consciousness" both do a good job of conveying the image that we exist in a sea of information.

That we are affected in various ways by the information in this soup should be quite obvious by now. It should also be obvious that we have taken a lot of the information in the cosmic soup personally. Understanding that how we relate/react to the information can and does create feelings of joy and happiness, pain and sadness can help us step out of a very old way of being in this world, into a very new way of being.

Our heart is a key player in the mystery of life, transmitting as it does complex songs to every cell in our being. Are we happy because the heart is singing happy songs? Or is the heart singing happy songs because we are happy? Happiness could be viewed as a condition where there are no land mines exploding in our system, no chemicals of discomfort being released into our body. But as long as we have denied any part of who we are, this happy state cannot last. The less shadow remains in our backpack, the longer and deeper we can remain in a state of bliss.

If any part of the heart is closed for repairs, shut down and unable to dance with all of the music in the cosmic soup, then we are only living a part of our potential. If the heart is limited in the songs it can sing to the other cells, then the chemicals that the body produces will also be limited in their range. If your heart isn't singing love songs, the chemicals the brain produces cannot be loving, healthy chemicals. If your heart is closed because of a misunderstanding way back in your past, then re-opening the heart for business should be a priority.

But trying to rush opening the heart is unlikely to work. In fact, it can cause more problems than you are attempting to resolve. Simply put, a healthy, fearless heart should be completely able to do the cosmic two-step with Shiva or with any other imaginable aspect of the divine. At the drop of a hat, it should be able to match and embrace any information it encounters.

Instead, it hides a part of itself away, hurt and frightened by misunderstandings, real or imagined. When it is asked to sing the scales, there are several flat notes because the charge around a situation held in your awareness does not want to reawaken the old feelings of hurt. When any external stimulus matches the frequency of the stored painful memory, sympathetic resonance triggers the memory, we lose control and re-experience the trauma. The cycle just keeps playing out, and the more we try and bury old, painful information, the stronger the charge that we create in the imbalance, and the more likely we are to have a serious confrontation in our attempt to resolve the imbalance.

This confrontation can manifest inwardly as physical health issues or an emotional or mental breakdown.

Outwardly, it can manifest as an explosion of violence or an attempt to manipulate or control the environment. By the time the charge has reached sufficient intensity to cause emotional or physical damage to others, there is no reasoning with the person as they lose themselves completely in reaction. It is not possible for them to see how they arrived at this place, as the very process of creating the potential for this to happen denies any personal responsibility, seeking always to blame others for the rage and frustration they feel. Rage and frustration are pretty extreme cases, used only to highlight where this inner imbalance can take us. Many of us are dealing with some level of imbalance, almost on a moment-by-moment basis, and the fact that we are not going into rage and frustration all the time is indicative only of the level of charge we hold or of our ability to still deny what is happening to us.

A partially or completely closed heart has the potential to destroy its host by failing to meet and share the information of its environment. In the struggle to maintain inner equilibrium, the person may continue to believe that even more control of their external environment is required. This belief only adds to the imbalance of the whole, justifying the individual's sense that outside factors were responsible for their state of discomfort or insecurity. Caught on a very destructive and not so merry merry-go-round, we fail to see the true cause for our insecurity and create even more problems for ourselves, others, and our environment.

Imagine just for a moment, that the cosmic soup, this sea of consciousness in which all life swims, is an electrical field. Within this field are many thousands of volts of information supercharging the soup. Imagine also your body, in particular, your heart as being highly sensitive pieces of manufactured electrical equipment. You were designed to be able to access the many thousands of volts flashing through the cosmic soup. But someone on the production line was having a bad day when you were put together. The result was that you were only able to deal with a few volts. You didn't know there was a problem with your equipment because the whole batch of bodies and hearts that were put together on the same production run as you were all faulty as well, so by default, everyone was in the same situation. Because your equipment is faulty, you can only access a limited number of those available volts of information, and you—along with everyone else, well, almost everyone else—think that this is all there is.

You forgot to bring the manual with you, and so did everyone else. As a result, there is nothing you can refer back to that will help you understand what is going on. So people start to make up their own manuals, deciding for themselves about the reality they are supposed to be in. This leads to some very interesting manuals (this one, for example!), which are often in conflict with other manuals. We could call this is one of the wonderful diversities of human nature, except where certain people believe that their manual is the only right one, and they try and sell it to others who were quite happy with their own manual. More conflict ensues as the other groups believe they have the right manual and resist the adoption of any other one.

It would be funny if it were not perilously close to the truth. It can also get very confusing, as there are so many manuals to choose from that people tend to believe that their parents' manual is good enough for them.

Most manuals work—to a point. If you don't question the validity of your manual, it will probably work for you till you die. Then it's crunch time. Time to find out if your manual was the one or not. Maybe there are/were some who questioned their manual and just maybe they went their own way and explored the human potential. Their numbers may have included people from all nations, all walks of life, all religious persuasions, all socio-economic backgrounds, all professions. And what if all those people started, independently of one another, to come to the same conclusion? Then that conclusion may be worth a second look.

I think that has happened and is happening as you read these words. I think the new manual is all about the heart and shows us ways that will help each of us to open our hearts more and more. This manual has, in fact, been around for a very long time. It has been analyzed and interpreted over the eons and diluted over time. The message has always been there, but we just have not had the ears to hear. If the heart had production run flaws but has always had the potential to access the full range of information, then we would be well served in rewiring it or doing whatever it takes to discover the true nature and potential of who we are supposed to be. This manual is also one that accepts all other manuals, not seeing one as better or worse than any other.

But opening up the heart all of a sudden to thousands of volts could be catastrophic, so we must be patient. We can open the heart little by little, giving our heart and our nervous system time to adjust, to adapt to a much bigger picture than we had previously held true. Where we are going on this journey may be beyond our imaginings, and this is yet another reason for patience. Opening up too much too quickly may put a huge strain on the nervous system, and, if there is still a lot of re-wiring required in that system, it could blow a circuit, causing the system to break down. Slowly, slowly, make sure your body and nervous system are comfortable with the increasing information before you seek more.

I often use the analogy of wanting to climb Mount Everest. Like many of us, someone might be impatient because they can only get two weeks vacation. So, wanting to stand on top of Everest, this person hires a helicopter to take them there. I doubt that a helicopter can actually fly that high, but we are pretending here anyway, so we may as well pretend that there is a helicopter that can. Stepping aboard the helicopter, dressed in T-shirt, shorts, and sandals, our adventurer may last 10 minutes on the top of Everest before lack of oxygen and the cold finish his adventuring days. Had he taken time, prepared properly, and worked slowly from one camp to another, by the time he reached the summit, his body would have acclimated to the conditions, and he would have lived to climb another day.

The same applies to the opening of the heart. We can certainly pretend, or even intend, to be compassionate, no matter the state of our heart, and we can still do things that will benefit others and ourselves. But if we cannot actually live in compassion, with every cell in our body hearing the song of love from the heart, then we are, in truth, transmitting a very different message.

I used to question my interpretation of the manual, I just could not accept on faith some of the views that presented in my awareness. I would try them out, apply them, and see if they worked, then slowly adopt or adapt them into my life. I never questioned whether my manual was the right one, the best one, or even whether it was relevant to others. Not because I assumed it was the right one or the best one, but it was just the one that I was drawn to and wanted to work with. If it helped others find their own manuals, wonderful, but I wasn't trying to sell it. I certainly questioned why I was drawn to this particular interpretation, to this path. Where had the desire or the knowing come from that was leading me down this particular path? I don't believe I am the sort of person who could stand up in front of room full of people and speak nonsense, but then, who does? We may well believe the words we speak as we speak them because they are, after all, expressions of who we are. Perhaps it would be more accurate to say, expressions of who we believe ourselves to be at that moment in time.

I ask people attending my workshops to not believe a word I say. That can be challenging for those who come seeking answers. You can see that they hear me, but many don't accept that I don't want them to believe me—not at first anyway. Many people tend to take me seriously because I am the one standing at the front of the room whilst everyone else is sitting. This is not a good enough reason to believe me. I tell people that I do not have the answers, yet it is in the nature of people who are seeking to keep finding new ways of asking the same question. They are seeking a definitive statement, something they can rest in for a while. They want someone to tell them, "This is how it is." I don't do this, I cannot do this, for I truly do not know how it is. All I can do is to share my own experiences. I have read other people's accounts of how it is, according to their perceptions at the time they wrote them down. Just because their point of view is in writing does not make it the truth. It may be one aspect of the bigger picture, but taken out of context and held up as something special, given more energy by those who read it, the words tend to take on more importance than they deserve.

Find out for yourself. I am just a guide along they way, sharing my journey, which may or may not help you for a part of your journey. At least I know that I do not know. Your personal knowing comes from your own experiences. Apply the knowledge, the wisdom, sort it out, accept what you can, leave the rest, and discover your truth for as long as it lasts. Then leave it behind and take the next step.

It is quite possible that what we are moving into is much more powerful than we have imagined possible. Indeed, how would it be possible for a heart that is limited in the information it can access to even begin to understand the bigger picture. To continue to identify with things as they currently appear to be, or as you have "known" them to be is not only limiting your own growth but limiting the growth of those around you.

The stepping stones as a path out of limitation that I mentioned earlier are like belief patterns that we use, and then discard once they have served their purpose. Each subsequent belief pattern is less limiting, less restrictive than the previous one. And then we let go of that one and move on into an even less restrictive belief. People have commented on the goal of this work as being one that is free of any particular belief. This does not mean that you believe in nothing, but rather that you are not attached to any one belief as being more right than any other. This non-attachment allows those neural synapses to respond to whatever presents without any preconditioning. I agree that non-attachment to any one belief system is a part of the journey. And I believe that while enlightenment may perhaps not be the end of the road as far as the full exploration of consciousness is concerned, it is very much a goal for those who practice this work.

I was once asked if our outer reality is really a manifestation of our inner aspirations, desires, conflicts, judgments, etc. and, if the goal is to reach enlightenment, why do we need to "dream a better reality." What is the point of dreaming a new dream when it is so easy to get lost in the dreaming once more and take the new dream for the reality, which, by its very nature, is not enlightenment.

My reply at the time was that I, too, expect the "dreaming" to stop for the individual once they are enlightened, however, not being enlightened, I cannot comment on what will happen at that point. (And whether the individual will still exist after enlightenment is yet another unanswered question.)

The reason I ask more people to change the dream and dream a better reality is to create better conditions, which will give others who are more lost in the illusion the opportunity to awaken to their true natures. As individuals wake up, so they create an expanding opportunity for others, who are lost in the dream, to see through the dream. And, of course, the more people awaken, the easier it becomes for others who follow, for if we were to continue dreaming what is for many a nightmare, then that will hold everyone in fear and confusion.

And as people discover the power of the dream, that they can change their personal dream, and that this will affect the collective dream, so they are encouraged to awaken a little more on this conscious journey to enlightenment and, in the process, create a better "reality" for them, their families, and their children's children.

If you become angry with others, it simply means that you are judging them, keeping them in a place of duality and more judgment, so you see, whenever you judge, you are a part of the problem, not the solution.

Your pessimism is also a product of the dream, and for a person who is in the process of awakening, this feeling of despair is quite common. Yet even if you are correct, and the majority who dream the dream of separation continue to do this for the next five million years, surely your own task is for you to reach the enlightened state. Until then, you really cannot help the rest very much, and then, once you are enlightened, you will be able to see through the drama, then you can decide whether it is time to move on or return as a boddhisatva and support others who are ready and willing to make the journey.

It can be difficult for those so lost to even begin to imagine that there is any other way of being. I believe that we can all learn of another way of being only when there is an example that we can see and follow, if we so choose. People who are becoming aware of both the need for another way of being and possible ways to bring that new way of being about, play an important role in facilitating change. They feed into greater clarity, greater love and compassion into the sea of consciousness, which, in turn, helps others who may not have even considered the possibility before. The results are exponential.

Yet for anyone to go straight from A to Z, is, as previously said, not realistic. It is not impossible, but not realistic. We cannot know the full extent of an individual's past, and if we truly are a product of our past, then the obstacles each of us face on this journey vary tremendously. Some may well find it easier to travel this road than others.

By slowly changing your personal view of the world and moving at a pace that you find comfortable and safe, you are learning to love yourself a little more each day, embracing the shadow side, and helping others find greater peace and safety. You are rewriting your history, so that tomorrow, your past will no longer be such a controlling influence in your life, as you have found a new way of relating to the inner you and the outer "environment."

The difference between this journey of introducing new belief patterns and supplanting older ones is that each consecutive belief is designed to be less and less restrictive. Many belief patterns are the opposite, setting quite limited options and futures for those who follow them.

Some may be concerned that by letting go of the past, by releasing attachment to or association with any thoughts or feelings, we will not experience any thoughts and feelings in the future. Quite the opposite is true. When we don't have any judgment around thoughts and feelings that arise, we experience a much broader range of thoughts and feelings. On a physical level, this occurs because, when we stop judging one thought or feeling to be better or worse than another, the heart no longer finds it necessary to attempt to block out that thought or feeling.

As the heart is made to feel safer by not identifying with or personalizing the information that was previously remembered as traumatic, it is opening up to receive more of the total transmission from the great cosmic soup. In it's turn, the brain is getting re-wired, old, conditioned neurological responses are being freed up to respond and not react. Though I am sure there are plenty of neurological responses we don't want to free up, for example, those that keep our system running effectively, what we do want to free up are any connections that prevent freedom of choice.

As the heart opens up to more and more information without taking it all so personally, and as the brain is re-wired, the ongoing need to continue to personalize everything that arises in one's awareness lessens. Think about the image of the backpack for a moment. One perceived goal is to empty the backpack, to be free once and for all of all shadow parts of the self. This is not really the goal of this work, but rather, the day-to-day practice is working at changing our relationship to the information stored in the backpack. This different way of relating to the energy stored in the backpack leads to a more open, trusting, and loving heart. It leads to old, fixed neurological reactions being freed up so they can respond more freely to information in the future. Another major benefit of changing our relationship to the shadow is that we stop, or at the very least, reduce the information we put into the backpack.

By developing the ability to not get lost in any of the thoughts and feelings, we can begin to feel safer as we experience a much broader range of feelings than previously. We develop new ways of handling situations, we find we can cope with life's challenges much more easily than before, in fact, a lot of the challenges cease to present because we no longer hold charge around them. We still feel, in fact, we feel more, but we no longer get quite so lost in the feeling.

To think that by not identifying with or non-attachment to thoughts and feelings is going to reduce the thoughts and feelings is simply not true. Yet these are just words, my words, and each of us needs to discover for ourselves whether these words resonate.

Another question that is often asked is, "If we are not our thoughts or our feelings, what are we?" This is not so easy to understand because, until we have at least begun to release attachment to what we believe to be our thoughts and our feelings, it is impossible to "know" what is beyond those old concepts. The structure that we held on to and associated with, by its very nature, denied access to the answer to that question. I don't think it is possible to know who you are while you still associate with thoughts and feelings. I believe that is why the Buddha told stories, Jesus told parables. No one can tell you who you are as long as you are still identifying with shadow because you will not believe it. You cannot even hear it. And you will not hear the message until you're ready. When you are ready it will be because your heart is fearless and your brain free to respond. Your past has prepared you for that moment, like preparing a field to receive the seeds. When you reach this stage, it all appears so obvious, so simple. The journey to this place, your history, has been what has created your current ability to see the world, whatever that may be. Each step you take along the way is just as important as all the others.

As you come to know—from your own experience— more of the true nature of who you are, it becomes more obvious that it is just not possible to understand the true nature of who you are while you are still lost in the drama of your personality, your likes and dislikes, your judgments.

It is not so much about telling anyone the answer anyway, it is about living it. People get moments of clarity, moments of insight, ah-ha moments throughout their lives. Normally, these moments do not last very long. They come and go in an instant, often leaving us wondering if they really happened or not. We get drawn back into the body, the personality very quickly and easily because the old conditioning quickly kicks in—a return to safe ground, or more accurately put, known ground. We cannot hold the insight because our past has not yet prepared us to be able to remain in this new understanding or clarity. When we become aware of our thoughts, possibly trying to understand the revelation we have just received, we start to follow that thought, expanding on it. When we do this, we are again lost in the mind's attempts to rationalize, and we have lost the moment.

So, another benefit of changing our relationship to the information stored in the backpack—or even emptying the backpack a bit—is that by reducing the charge, we are able to remain longer in the moment of clarity.

If it is true that we create our reality, not by our desires or our positive affirmations but by the totality of who we are, the shadow self included, then it is easy to see why there is so much conflict in the world today. Many people certainly do not live in a particularly safe or peaceful world. Where legislation is required just so that people will get along is a sign that any significant change is going to require a fundamental shift in thinking. If, on a very basic level, we are contributing to the current state of affairs with little or no conscious effort, by simply being who we are, then it is understandable why, on a more conscious level, there appears to be so much to fix. Unconsciously, our shadow manifests, and we then try and fix the results. How we continue to relate to ourselves and others supports the ongoing creation of the current view we have of the world, which is obviously in conflict with some other points of view.

Exercise

For a start, we should realize that experiencing an emotion is not going to kill us, it may seem like it at the time, but in reality, we are just going through the results of certain chemicals, which have been released into our system. The next time you feel a very strong emotion, take a step back from it and remember that this is what it is. And don't forget to breathe.

The sooner we can understand this, the sooner we can change the manifesting reality. Remember, once you are lost in the emotion, you have lost control, and it is very difficult to be objective about that emotional energy. Sit quietly and practice tuning in to situations and emotions, notice how it feels, understand that the feeling is really the result of a chemical process, which you can ultimately learn to control.

Chapter Eleven
Dreaming a World into Being

The indigenous Australian people have a belief that they refer to as the Dream Time. They believe that each tribe needs to keep dreaming the dream of their tribe in order for their reality, the integrity of their tribe to be maintained. There are many different dreamings, each playing its part in holding together the local cultures. They believed that if they should ever stop dreaming the dream, then their world, their "worldview" would fall apart and cease to be. And that, to a large extent, is what is happening now. They didn't stop dreaming the dream by choice, but they began to stop dreaming the dream after Europeans colonized their land. Over the years, their culture was undermined so that now the young are no longer dreaming the dream. The young no longer follow in the footsteps of their elders. You can see this as progress or genocide, depending upon which "side" you take.

This behavior of imposing a different set of beliefs upon an existing, indigenous culture has been a popular approach to colonization for millennia. As a new culture overlays its values, its belief systems on another, the pre-existing culture is undermined. The dreaming changes, and the reality changes with it.

Although the majority of us do not call what we are doing "the dreaming" we are nonetheless, dreaming our dream. We are dreaming our world into being, but, unlike the indigenous Australians who knew what they were doing and why, we are not aware of the full significance of our creative abilities.

We may have a sense that we have lost our connection to god, to self, to something outside of us. Throughout history it seems to have been humankind's lot to feel they have lost something and to then spend all their time on earth looking for it. For the most part we externalize that search. During the process of seeking, we further validate the charge or the belief that we are looking for something and that the answer is "out there." We actually increase the charge by trying to fix the external around us.

While the majority of people who are lost in separation, lost in isolation, lost in fear, lost in suffering, all feed back their pain, their suffering, their lack into the cosmic soup, they will continue to co-create a worldview that appears to be lacking, reflecting their own inner imbalance. This is their dream, or should I say nightmare? Their manifesting worldview may be one that is lacking in love, in support, in financial wealth, in food, in shelter, in joy, in whatever. When we see that we are supporting this worldview by holding on to our personal beliefs about what is possible and what is not, by our continued denial of the shadow self, we begin to recognize that we are a part of the problem. And with that recognition comes a way out.

One avenue open to those feeling dispossessed or unheard in the past has been a revolution. Social revolutions have never really changed the world on any fundamental level, they just exchange one set of beliefs for another. Unfortunately the "new" beliefs are still within the old paradigm or framework. They cannot be otherwise, since the people who took part in the revolution are still, intrinsically, following the same fundamental belief patterns of those they were in revolt against.

People who seek to improve their lot in life are limited to work through commonly accepted avenues, legal or not. To imagine that there could be any way outside of the current consensus or way of viewing the world is so "out there" that even though we may try and break free from the collective expectations, the infrastructure to support any different way is just not there. We easily fall back on the old time-worn ways, even though they have not truly served us well in the past. Better the devil you know ...

If we can't find the peace in our current paradigm, in our house, in our country, there aren't many options for the majority. If we are "lucky" we can go and find another place or situation and hope that our prayers will be answered. The excitement or distraction of the new may keep us entertained for a little, but after a while it is the same-old-same-old because, basically, nothing has changed. Sooner or later, when our past catches up with us, we move on, still searching for the peace we think is out there. But still we are putting out the same old transmission. We can run from our shadow, but we never escape it.

This is why our main aim should not be to empty the backpack. As long as we still have any judgments, fears, or denied past, we will always attract and associate with more shadow, refilling the backpack with one hand as the other empties it. Better to change our relationship to the information stored in the backpack. That way, over time, the information stored in the backpack becomes more and more meaningless, and the aspects of personality that allowed charge to build are no longer there, so nothing gets added.

Over the years, as I have been sharing the information contained in this book in my workshops, I have changed. It is just not possible to keep sharing this and remain who you used to be. A big part of that change has been a growing awareness of the shadow. I no longer see a lot the shadow as mine, after all, as I let go of attachment to likes and dislikes and judgments, the shadow has released whatever hold it had on me. I cannot say that I am no longer at the mercy of any shadow, for there are certainly areas of which I am not aware, areas where the shadow is still very strong. All I can say is that as I understand this more, then slowly I am able to embrace more of "my" shadow. It is a journey, and the goal, whatever and wherever that may be, is not important.

I am still influenced by my past, what happened to me, and how I reacted, but now I recognize that the shadow is all of the unloved aspects of the collective, not the individual. It is just how, through our personal journey, we have associated with the information in the past.

Another personal benefit, as I travel this road, is the realization that, from a very early age, I have been extremely sensitive. Being very sensitive may not be seen by all as beneficial, especially those who have little or no control over their sensitivity. As a child I learned to control—or perhaps a better word here would be deny—my sensitivity in order to survive what I must have considered a hostile environment. This path has given me the opportunity to begin to open up, to feel safe once more and to get in touch with many feelings. You may think this is good or not, but seeing physical and emotional dis-ease as, in a large part, the product of inner imbalance and stress, I personally feel any denied emotional energy is much better discharged than stored in the backpack, moldering away. Another associated realization has been that many of the feelings I have felt and been overpowered by in the past had absolutely nothing to do with me. I personalized those feelings, strongly identifying with them because I knew no other way to work with them. This did not mean that they were mine originally. I made them mine by taking them personally. Having made them mine, the painful ones were pushed aside to take their place in the infinite space of my backpack.

I may still struggle a little believing some of the stronger memories and feelings are mine. The conditioning we experience as a child can be very powerful, and there are parts of my early conditioning that I cannot even look at without real trouble, never mind letting go of them. Yet as we tread the path and practice not taking personally that which arises in the present moment, we are also learning to get in touch with other, deeper feelings—those hidden at the bottom of the backpack. Community is an important part of the journey. As we begin to realize that the information stored as shadow is just information and should really exert no control over our actions and decisions in the now, having friends who support this realization helps us to move beyond the old limitations and fears.

Yet another benefit for many who travel this path is the realization that there can be no blame. Practicing non-judgment makes a big difference to the energy we attract into our lives, but recognizing that each and every one of us is equally lost in the drama of our collective making helps us cultivate our non-judgment. We come to understand that everyone, without exception, has done and is doing, the best they can. That is often hard to imagine when we look outside and see so much that we perceive as chaos and abuse. Yet, when we understand that each and everyone of us is a product of our past, each having our own genetic inheritance, our own soul memory, our own social conditioning, it is not so difficult to realize that each one of us does the best we can, given the circumstances. I think this is what Jesus meant when he reportedly said, "Judge not, lest ye be judged." We just cannot even begin to imagine why people are as they are, why they do what they do. We can no longer blame our parents for a poor job in raising us, we cannot blame our siblings, our bosses, our politicians. We cannot blame anyone at all.

My openness, my personal sensitivity in the past had taken on the energy of the people and the environment and been overwhelmed by it all. Without any conscious awareness on my part, I became a little of everyone and everything in my world. Without knowing it, I had few personal boundaries and, in relationship, became or merged with the personality of the other person. A big part of my challenge was just to realize that this had happened.

For many years, I had no idea that this was what was happening to me. Instead, after being close to someone for a short while, I would lose whatever it was I had imagined myself to be, merging with the personality of the other person. I don't think this is a good way to be in relationship because it is as though you sell yourself out in order to be with the other person. Meanwhile, the other person takes a dislike to you because you are no longer the person they thought they were in relationship with. You have become a mixture of your own conditioning and theirs. This has the effect of you becoming the shadow side of the others' personality and reflecting it back to them. This was happening to me a lot, not just in intimate relationships, but with friends and business associates as well. When I was alone, I was myself, at least I thought I was myself. Looking back now, I cannot be sure of who the self is. Another important side effect of losing myself this way was that I ended up not liking this me. Not liking this "new" me, I would blame it on the person I was merging with. Try and extricate yourself from that situation. As I mentioned earlier, the biggest challenge was to even be aware of the fact that I was losing myself, for, without awareness, there is no real resolution. Instead I/we would try and resolve the differences that were arising from within the "lost-ness" of the evolving situation. A total nightmare.

Does this happen to everyone? Is this common? I have no trouble accepting that humanity is connected in consciousness. My experiences in this area have been too many and too varied to not accept this. Because of this largely unacknowledged connection, I can also see how easy it would be for individuals to take on characteristics of others, without being aware they are doing so.

Is it possible that even those of us with a "strong" personality are being affected, on some level or another, by everyone around them? We may wish to hold on to the idea that we are separate, isolated beings, but we cannot deny we are being affected by a huge range of information, information that we believe to be external, every moment of our lives. To what degree we are being affected remains to be seen.

There has been, for me, a plus side of this personality, or better perhaps to say this growing lack of personality. That is the awakening to the reality that the confusion of thoughts and feelings I once thought were mine are not mine. This has been—and still is—very liberating. It may or may not have been a weakness on my part that made me lose myself in the personality of those around me, but that is no longer important. I recognize that—like a chameleon—I was adapting to ever changing environments. Yet another survival tool to add to denial!

The reason for my taking on so much of another could have been due more to an absence of any strong identification with a personality of my own than any weakness. I know that this lack of identification with any fixed personality has helped me when I stand in front of a group of people to share this understanding. I have seen the results of someone with a strong attachment to personality teaching, and you can feel the opposition in the room, bubbling up to the surface. You can see people are just not getting the message. Many have gone into an unconscious reaction to the personality that is trying to "tell" them how it is. To me, and I am sure most of those who have studied with me will agree, my lack of attachment to personality creates a much softer, less threatening situation. This allows those present to easily assimilate the information because the parts of their personalities that would have been sensitive to anything in the way of dogmatic personality that I might have brought into the room with me have not been awakened. This is not to say that I don't trigger any shadow issues for people in workshops—I do. But at the same time, I am creating or holding a heart space for them to see and move through that charge held in their shadow.

To be free of any concept of the self whatsoever, would, according to the words of the Buddha, equal an enlightened state. It has been reported that the Buddha said that attachment to any concept of the self was the last thing to let go of before enlightenment—and the hardest. I make no claim to be anywhere near that state. I know I still get caught up in shadow. But I am also coming to know more and more that that shadow is not mine, it is just shadow. The collective dark side. So, Luke Skywalker, embrace the dark side, and it will have no power over you ever again. Fight it, and it will be your constant companion. An interesting idea, and, until you try it, you will never know just how powerful and liberating it can be.

It is interesting to take a look at how the dark side has been represented throughout history and how fear and denial have created and helped maintain the dark side. The more power we as individuals give to the dark side, externalizing, yet again, our fears and the hidden aspects of self, the stronger it grows. Given enough energy through the beliefs of enough people, then that which we fear—or have yet to confront personally—will actually manifest in the world, proving the nature of our co-creative ability.

It may be difficult to see just how that shadow is manifesting because we are so used to it being out there in the world that this is how we believe the world to be. It has always has been like that, at least according to our history books. And if it is out there, then we have to react to it. That is the way of the world, after all. Yet if we could but see that reacting to the manifestation is a part of the cause that created it in the first place, then perhaps we would stop for a moment and reflect upon what is really going on. Then, instead of reacting, we might see another way to be in the world. Simply because we believe that is how things are, does not make it true. The more we apply this different way of being, the more we understand that we are indeed co-creating the dream into reality and the more we are empowered to change the dream.

When we can see how our shadows are manifesting in the world, the door opens for an alternative way of dealing with those shadows. We discover a way that the shadow can be dealt with before it manifests. I referred earlier to the work of Arnold Mindell, about stepping outside of time, becoming edgeless. As you reach this awareness and ability, you will not even see the manifestation of your shadow. That which was holding the potential to manifest a situation of stress or discomfort, an aspect of your shadow, no longer has any charge or power over you because you have loved it in yourself.

Whilst we continue to deny the existence of the shadow and work at trying to fix the problem from within that place that created the problem in the first place, then Mindell's words "... Such moments require a lot of awareness, personal courage and flexibility," will hold true because we are still challenged by the issues that confront us and take them very seriously. By acknowledging and exploring the shadow, we can see that those manifesting issues are, in part, a product of our own conscious and subconscious beliefs and expectations. The next step would be to change our relationship to those beliefs and expectations. As we do this, they cease to manifest, and we do not have to deal with them on a physical level. This is an interesting concept when applied to the health of the individual. It is so much easier to deal with issues on an energetic level than it is to wait until they manifest physically. Because most of us wait until those issues become physical and manifest as sickness or dis-ease, we have to resort to physical intervention in an attempt to bring balance back. To deal with issues on an energetic level requires a certain amount of awareness and self-responsibility, yet the current collective paradigm includes little awareness of this and rejects self-responsibility.

For each and everyone of us who has any imbalance manifesting in their lives, be it on a physical internal or external level, emotional, mental, financial, whatever, accepting responsibility for this does not necessarily mean that you created it. Why would anyone in their "right" mind create poverty or sickness? Why would anyone volunteer as the underdog. You, the co-creator of your world, may have no recollection or understanding of where the cause for any manifesting imbalance could have come from. At this stage of the journey, it is not important to understand this, although some people feel it is. They believe that by understanding why something is happening, they will move beyond the limitations their lack of understanding is imposing upon them. I do not think it is realistic to expect people to easily understand the cause of manifesting imbalance. The energy that has created the current reality is so embedded in the essence of who they perceive themselves to be that to question the foundations upon which their life has been built is just too far outside the box. It is not going to happen without a new way of seeing the self.

By continuing to give energy to the perceived problem, by looking for and working with potential cause, we are saying to ourselves, "I have a problem, and I must work hard at solving that problem." Even allowing that there is some truth to this statement, if we think about this for a moment, we can see how, by our continued identification with the perceived problem, we are giving it power. The more power we give it, the more we have to do to overcome it. This is happening on both personal and global levels.

What happens when we take the power away from the "problem" is that the energy that was being devoted to maintaining a particular state is redirected. The redirected energy may or may not heal that manifestation of imbalance. Although that may happen, success depends on how long the body has identified with the imbalance. The more we have conditioned ourselves, subconsciously, to believe something to be the truth, the more likely it is to manifest physically. The more physical an issue becomes, the harder it is to convince yourself, your subconscious, that this is not how things are. Even though you may not experience immediate relief from symptoms every time you redirect your energy and your awareness, you are slowly rewiring the brain, thereby allowing for other possibilities.

I am not a great believer in positive affirmations, and this is not what I am suggesting here. I think that whilst any shadow lies hidden and unexamined, positive affirmations tend to create a more polarized internal conflict between what you want and what you have. I am not even suggesting you go exploring the dark side, but simply that you begin to change your relationship with yourself. To attempt to change the relationship to self on our own, with no previous experience or awareness may not be the easiest way to go, but we can make a start. Positive affirmations may work if you are able to get in touch with areas of the self you are not comfortable with and begin to make changes to how you react to those situations. If you continue to deny the shadow and always seek the happy solution, then you may well be creating an even greater charge than existed before.

Accepting responsibility does not mean you are to blame. This has often been said in the past, and is something that prevents many people from exploring the self in this way.

Nor is accepting responsibility a judgment of you or your past. Remember, we all do the best we can in the circumstances given our past. Accepting responsibility for where you are now is simply opening a door to a whole new way of being. If I am responsible for what is happening to me now, then I can change whatever I need to in order to live a happier, more abundant life. If I am not responsible, then I must look outside for who or what is, and then lobby, petition, pray to whoever I have given power to and hope my petitions and my prayers are heard. I wish you luck if you for a moment imagine that a politician will solve the ills of the world, they bumble along like the rest of us, caught in the drama, trying to manipulate and control the drama for the benefit of one group.

Even just pretending for a moment that we are responsible for creating our current worldview, which Erwin Schrödinger seemed to believe was truly the case, these realizations give us the power to begin to explore other options towards greater health and happiness. We may begin by asking ourselves, why we created such a life. A big question, and, if you try and work that one out from your current awareness, it may rob you of the next 5 or 10 years of your life. Looking for answers is not going to help. You may discover an answer, but if you could be objective about that answer, you might well find that you have selected something that supports your current worldview or your perceptions of your self. So you are able to further justify your thoughts, words, and deeds by the logic of the rational mind. This is not really going to help you step into any self-empowerment or find resolution, as it is still justifying your externalization of a denied shadow side.

Rather than try and find a reason for why you are who you think you are, and why what happens to you happens as it does, simple acceptance will lead to the answers you are looking for.

Exercise

Think about your past and how that past has brought you to where you are now. Notice how decisions made, consciously or otherwise, have created the world that you live in now. See how situations, seemingly out of your control, have contributed to your life as it now appears to be. When you can view your life a little more objectively, it is easier to accept responsibility for your past, for everything that is in your backpack, for your shadow. Remember, this has nothing to do with blame. As you are able to see how your past has created the present, you will also understand how the present is creating your future. Once you can do that, you can begin to consciously change your mind, in the moment and take whatever steps you need to take to dream a new future—one that is less limited by the past.

Chapter Twelve
Living Outside the Box

Let's take a moment here to talk about the box in which we find ourselves, the box of our personality. Everyone on earth has a box they call the body, it houses the spirit, the soul, or whatever words we use to refer to the divine, eternal aspect of who we are. So we all have something in common. The fact that the boxes, or bodies, are divided into two major categories, female and male, and all have different shapes, colors, sizes has been a source of conflict for a very long time. Interesting when you think about it, how association with one model puts you into conflict with other models. Irrespective of your sex or skin color, you have other aspects that you identify with.

Recapping some of the earlier observations here, you have your genetic memory, soul memory, cultural identity, language, etc., which are a part of the foundation of the personality. This is the skeleton or frame upon which you hang the clothes of your developing personality. Your likes and dislikes, your values, your hopes and expectations, your fears all interweave and become the personality, who you think yourself to be. We can easily visualize this as a box where you can fit all the parts that you think are you. As long as information fits within the box, it is something you can handle, something you find easy to accept. So it is not so difficult to imagine that any answers you seek to any questions you may imagine can only be acknowledged or accepted by you if they fit within your current worldview. Your box.

Most of us have heard the saying "think outside the box." Assuming we can find a reason to do so, how can we do that? You need to find your own reasons. Mine are that whilst I remain in the box, I am limited, I am subject to those limitations, and I can only expect more of the same in the future. I can find no answers to whatever may be troubling me from within the box, for it was being in the box that created the troubles in the first place. Reason enough for me to want to explore the edges of the box and look for ways out of the limits it imposes upon me.

We can also imagine that the information stored within the center of box contains those aspects of self we have lovingly embraced. Everything on the fringe, around the inside edge of the box is information that we have either denied or have yet to embrace—our shadow. The information that is beyond the edges is so beyond our capacity to understand and embrace that we cannot even begin to imagine what it is. For most people, dealing with the personal shadow is enough of a challenge, and that which is totally unknown—beyond the box—is not even on the radar of their awareness. Given our current collective worldview, whatever is outside the box can stay there. Thinking outside the box is reduced to an intellectual exercise, such as, lateral thinking and coming up with new ways to solve old problems. This may add to the wisdom of humanity, and there have certainly been some great minds that had the capacity to think outside the box, however, the problem for those still in the box is that any information coming from outside is not very digestible.

If we come back to the benefits of changing our relationship to our self, to the box we have become attached to, we can see that the very concept of the box is just that, a concept. Yet to those in the box, this idea is incomprehensible and so far out of the box as to be meaningless. We quickly dismiss ideas or concepts that are outside of our box by either going into denial or by going into a very irrational reaction.

What makes any box better or worse than any other? How can one person in their personal or collective box judge another's personal or collective box? If you are in a box, you are in the same boat as everyone else. You either try and find resolution to your problems from within your box and create more conflict with those who live in different boxes, or you look outside the box. But for the reasons outlined above, not too many people do that.

Seeing the box as a concept and seeing how various people, so lost in their box, want to tell others about the joys of their own box, or perhaps convince them to trade their old box for one of these new ones, we can see how the world has developed as it has. If my concept contains lack or if it is fear-based and needs a lot of riches to make it feel happy and safe, then I will be justified in taking anything from anyone to satisfy those needs. I can even get god to justify my actions—a good trick if you can get away with it. It all comes down to what you believe.

A box can be a nice safe place for a while, as long as no one comes knocking at the door, selling extensions, or perhaps wanting to renovate your old box, or, heaven forbid, demolish it to make way for a highway. Your box can appear an even safer place if you get lots of others to subscribe to some of your fundamental beliefs. Then you have a religion, or a cult, or a political party, or some other kind of group. The more people who believe the same things as you, the more powerful your group becomes. Most groups are devoted to power, and getting more subscribers is one way of maintaining that power base. And so a concept becomes a reality.

When you stop subscribing to a belief pattern, some resistance from others within the belief pattern is likely. For those who still believe in a concept, that is a natural reaction when they look around and see their world falling apart. Sooner or later though, they will get over it, history has demonstrated that. Belief patterns come and they go. Not always in pleasant ways, and, more often than not, the resistance to change that certain groups feel results in open conflict. Whatever that concept was, it will fade back into the cosmic soup from whence it came, remembered in the history books, and for a while, in the stories and minds of some, till even that fades. As often happens, beliefs or concepts get distorted with the telling over time until they bear little resemblance to the belief pattern from which they were born. This distortion is not really important, as the "original" belief pattern was based on an earlier story, which in all likelihood was already distorted.

To challenge the reality of another person or group is asking for trouble. To claim that any one reality is better or worse than any other is to come from a place of judgment. If someone tries to tell me that my reality has a few problems and then proceeds to tell me how to fix them, there are a few ways I can react. What they are doing is asking me to step outside my comfort zone and embrace a way of being or a belief that is contrary to what I am convinced of as being the "right" way. This intrusion is most often met with an equal and opposite resistance on my part, which will, if the pressure is kept up, lead to conflict.

Storming the walls of another's box guarantees that the result will not be lasting happiness for all concerned. Recognizing that to even mention that someone is lost in their own personality and describe that personality as a box is asking for trouble. So what can we do?

I think we need to see that there is only one person on the planet we ultimately have responsibility for—ourself. Realizing that the current values, beliefs, and perceptions held by that self are transitory and that they were built on presumptions formed at best on very shaky ground is an important part of the journey. In truth, the only person we can "do" anything about is ourselves. We may want to try and fix others, but as long as we come from our personal limitations we cannot help another in the long term. When we try and fix others from within our personality, all we do is look at the other through the limited eyes and capacity of that personality and then impose the perceptions of the limited self upon another. This tends to create an even more confused state, one that requires more fixing. Around and around we go.

As we redirect our energy inwards and heal ourselves, the message that we transmit from our heart to our cells, to others, and to our environment is one of greater balance. Little by little, we project a more whole, healthy picture and, little by little, the universe responds to the changes occurring within us. As we spoke of earlier, if you don't realize that you are in a box or don't understand the part you play in co-creating your reality, then there is nothing to be done—other than change your doctor, your political party, your bank, your whatever.

By taking the first step toward recognizing the part that each of us plays in creating and supporting any worldview, we are moving toward a place of much greater empowerment. The first step is just one of many, and we cannot even imagine the second step until we have made the first, let alone see the goal. So to even begin the journey, there either has to be a lot of faith in someone or something, or there has to be a great desire to move beyond the bounds of the old. If faith is what motivates you or gives you the courage to move beyond the known, then as you progress down the path, that faith will have to be replaced with personal knowing, or one day you may find yourself out on a limb with no apparent way back.

It is easy, for a while, to have faith in something external to the self. The day will come, though, when the shadow can no longer be denied, and if you have not even begun to make friends with your dark side, this can be a very unsettling time. The meeting with and the acceptance of aspects of the shadow has often been called the dark night of the soul. When your past arises in your awareness with little or no preparation on your part, the previously denied emotions can be overpowering. This is why many of the spiritual traditions suggested that you have a guide, or, at the very least, a map, so that you knew where you were and could find your way back if you needed to.

I imagine, it could be likened to someone taking an hallucinogenic drug. I am not sure, but it seems to me that the drug opens the door of the subconscious, and if you have personal demons still hidden away, the drug is an invitation for them to come out and play. If you have dealt with much of your shadow, or you did not have a lot to begin with, then you would have what could be described as a "good trip." If you still had some serious dark-side issues, and you took mind altering drugs, watch out—this would be a "bad trip."

Many people manage their dark sides by continuing to deny they even have a shadow. For others, there can be so much charge that the shadow manifests, out of control, in their lives. If, as I believe, we are all products of our past, then it is all relative, and the dark side is also a product of that past. Ours and our ancestors. This should not be so difficult to accept. When you think about it, it is harder to believe that we are not products of the past.

By our continued identification with the body and the personality, the shadow is re-created moment by moment. The shadow is, after all, just a memory that you continue to take personally—how, for better or for worse, you or your ancestors have dealt with an event or experience in the past. It is in taking the memory personally, either holding it as true or denying it, that creates the charge around that memory that we are calling the shadow. The more we or society have judged an experience, the more charge there will be around that memory. This applies to "good" memories as well as "bad" ones. We can be a victim of our good memories as much as of our dark ones. It is good to remember here that we have not done anything wrong. Taking experiences personally has been a natural part of the human experience. Losing ourselves to a transitory identity is also a part of the program. Almost like a computer game, the player takes on the character they are playing, gets involved and lost in the game, forgets time and space and chores and work. It is as though we have stepped onto a stage or into a television program and play our part so well that we convince ourselves and everyone around us that we are indeed that character.

The difficulty lies in recognizing that this is what is happening because we are so deeply involved in the drama, so convinced that it is real. Even if we were to recognize this to be the case, what alternatives are there for us? At the moment not many, and most of those currently on offer are essentially just more of the same in a different costume. Much like the little carpet squares, we move from one to another in the search for a carpet that is just right for us.

Throughout history there always have been people who have believed their carpet to be the one and only way to peace, salvation, security, harmonious living. They tried hard to get others to subscribe and buy one of their carpets, and so it goes. I am not a carpet salesman, in fact, if I could, I would buy the carpets back, but to leave people carpet-less would, in their present state of mind, not be a kind thing to do. Perhaps it really is better then to pick at a thread of the carpet and just keep pulling away, slowly, gently, maintaining at all times a sense of safety and belonging.

If you begin this journey of questioning the validity of your carpet—and everyone else's as well—you are a brave person. You will appear to swim in the opposite direction to the rest of humanity. But hey, if all the salmon are swimming upstream to spawn and die, or the lemmings are rushing, unknowingly, to their end over the cliff, then perhaps swimming in the opposite direction is not such a bad thing after all.

This is all it takes, a moment to question everything that you have ever been told. Start with the little things. Discovering the meaning of life can wait a little longer.

Assume for a moment that what the Tibetan Buddhists say about forgetting the true nature of the self when you are born is true. This would help explain why, throughout history, there has been such a compelling desire among humankind to get an answer to the big question, "What the heck am I doing here? Again." It is more a search for a greater identity, a sense of belonging. Most people get their sense of belonging from the community into which they are born. But it seems that, for many people, the search for a greater self and for answers to the big questions has been externalized. Human awareness, limited as it is by its association with the body and the personality, cannot possibly grasp the enormity of its true nature. So, as they look for answers, people have handed all responsibility over to a god or gods. When people create gods, they must also create their equal and opposite numbers, the devil or devils. The yin and the yang of our physical reality—it doesn't seem as though you can have one without the other.

Now that is food for thought—that you can't have one without the other. If there were no "external" devil, how could humanity justify the evil acts they commit? If the devil is a creation of the human mind, which in turn is an extension of the shadow aspects of self, it follows that there is no devil. And then we are going to have to accept responsibility for our own shadow and stop blaming external influences. I guess it pretty much depends upon which god or gods you currently believe in, or which interpretation most comfortably fits your current worldview that dictates how much time and energy you give to the devil.

I was asked to work with a young girl many years ago. She was experiencing periods of what was being diagnosed as schizophrenia. She was apparently being "taken over" by a dark, malignant energy. Modern medicine called it schizophrenia, some religions would have said that she was possessed. Both have different ways of working with such manifestation. I saw it as a cry for help. An aspect of the child's shadow side was so strong, had so much charge, that it was manifesting as physical and verbal abuse through the child. If you believe in god, there is a chance you will believe in the devil. If a person experiences moments when they seem to lose control and become dark or negative and commit "evil" acts, then it is easy to blame it on the devil.

If you don't believe in the devil, then this is not a case of possession by a demonic force that needs exorcising. Schizophrenia may or may not be caused by a neurological "imbalance." No matter whether there is neurological cause for the schizophrenia or not, the neural networks are still contributing to the creation of an individual's reality. Into this mix goes an awareness that neural connections may be inherited from genetic ancestry or from soul memory. Any manifestation of "negative" patterning can be a product of inner turmoil, an externalization of the shadow's charge, whether it is caused by neural imbalance or something else.

It may also be that the brain because of the way it is wired, is more susceptible to some information or frequencies of thought and feeling than it is to other frequencies. Even before a person, whose neural links are triggered by certain frequencies, encounters that frequency as information in its perceived external environment, the potential for reaction already exists. It is then just a matter of the neurons in the brain going into a conditioned response to this particular stimulation and flooding the body with a chemical cocktail. What manifests may appear to be "possession," or schizophrenia, or multiple personality disorder, or obsession, or anger, or love, or whatever. Another person could be subject to the same external influences and be affected in a completely different way or have no reaction whatsoever, yet that same person may react strongly to other information.

I am not trying to say that any of the above was the reason for the child's experiences, just that maybe one of these possibilities was instrumental in the disturbed behavior patterns. I really do not know what was the original cause of this manifesting imbalance. It was not really important to me to know, and it wasn't important to either the child or the parents. The important thing was to resolve this imbalance without medication and certainly without a fear-based ritual.

It has become my understanding that by developing the ability to embrace a charge as it presents, the charge will, in effect, be neutralized. This is how I was able to help the young girl. By not judging what was happening or personalizing the feelings or thoughts that presented, by not running away from or trying to control the feelings or thoughts that arose, the charge was released. Quite simply by embracing the charge in my own heart, it lost its power. It was brought into a balanced state, was loved to the point where it was no longer perceived as an external force troubling the child, but once again an integrated part of who she was. To the degree that I was able to embrace her shadow, or what was being perceived as her shadow, I was instrumental in allowing her the opportunity to no longer go into a fear reaction or get lost in the experience. So, in effect, she was re-wiring her brain.

Because it had not gone into fear or any judgment of its own, my heart was holding the space for the child so that she momentarily found herself in a safe place. When the heart perceives itself to be safe, when the information it is picking up is not threatening, or it is not being reminded of an old, painful memory, it can meet the frequency of the information with love instead of fear. We call this opening the heart, and the child's open heart can then, at last, embrace the shadow aspect that had been manifesting as an abusive child.

This was many years ago, and there has been no recurrence of schizophrenic behavior. It is not always the case that such imbalance is so simply resolved, but it is always worth trying.

All of the above could be difficult if your conditioning is fear based, or if you continue to identify with or personalize whatever arises in your awareness. Fear is a product of a closed mind and a closed heart, and identifying with whatever you experience carries the risk of your becoming that which you identify with. Reason enough to run from that which you do not understand.

If you were to believe in the devil and possession, then you would have handled the situation with the child in a very different way. By believing in the devil or evil, you are actually giving it power, enabling its manifestation. Sounds crazy, why would anyone do that? Remember though that we are all coming from identification with the body, with the personality, lost in genetic memory, and, according to the Buddhist teachings, we have forgotten who we are. Besides, the most common way of dealing with the dark side in the past has been to externalize it.

For the most part, we are not even aware that we are doing this. Perhaps if we were aware, we would stop it.

Many years ago, I had a phone call from a young woman living in Queensland. Happily married, with two young babies, she had been having terrifying experiences with the youngest baby. Every time she would take the baby out onto the veranda at the back of the house, she would hear a voice telling her to throw the child off the veranda. The veranda was very high, the ground falling away steeply beneath it.

This had been happening for some time before she called me, in fact, the situation had become terrifying. I imagine that what prompted the call to me was the day everything went crazily out of control. She had just come inside from the veranda and had a feeling that she was being followed. She turned and saw a manifestation of her worst nightmare—a demonic shape that filled the high-ceilinged room. That was when she really lost it.

You might think that she was imagining this, and you are probably correct. Did she see this with her eyes or in her mind? But it really doesn't matter. That she saw it is enough. Whether others see it or not doesn't make it any more or less real to her. It was real enough to her at the moment, and it was terrifying. Similar to the young girl and the "schizophrenia," my understanding is that it was a manifestation of an imbalance, in this case an insecurity or fear. And when this imbalance was given enough energy, over time it manifested even if it were just in the young woman's mind. It is not good enough to try and convince her that this was not real; it was very real to her. A typical reaction that could be expected was for the person to think they are going crazy, and given enough support, that idea could well manifest.

To see the manifestation as a large charge being released is very liberating. Though it may have been easier all round if the charge had been released before it manifested. Seeing the disturbance this way, I was able, over a period of two weeks, to gradually embrace more and more of this woman's shadow. Perhaps more correctly put, I was able to hold an open heart, which then allowed her heart to find a place of safety from which it could itself embrace the shadow that had manifested in such a terrifying way. It's a story with a happy ending—shadow released, charge all gone, no more frightening manifestations.

Looking at these two examples of inner conflict or denied shadow, we can see how they may manifest as either schizophrenic behavior or as an almost physical presence. From there, it does not require much of a leap of imagination to extend the possibilities and see how our world or our view of the world is a product of our mind.

It may also be possible now to understand how any charge that manifests is one way that energy tries to find a place of balance. If order cannot be restored internally, then it attempts to do so externally. We have taken much of the external as real instead of seeing it as an expression of internal conflict.

It is apparent to me that all expressions of the self are nothing but energy seeking balance. I also believe that all systems seek a return to balance. We, with our human limitations, think we know what balance is or what balance means to our limited personality, and we try and impose those limitations on our environment. More often than not, we get in our own way and make life so much more difficult for ourselves than it need be. Our arrogance could be our worst enemy.

The energy that was creating the so-called schizophrenic behavior in the young girl was not trying to take over or possess her, though we could have seen it that way. Had we chosen to view this as a case of some demonic energy trying to take control of the girl, we would have, by our very acceptance of that belief, given some power to the energy that was expressing itself through the child. And by giving energy to the charge from our own beliefs and fears, we would have given it a place in our reality. Having done that, we would then need to do something about it.

In the past, and perhaps still in some places today, various rituals have been used to drive the "demon" from the person. To the degree the person performing the ritual is polarized between good and bad, light and dark, their fears and their judgments, the energy they are trying to move will often hold an equal and opposite charge. The more polarized the people involved in the ritual, the more polarized the energy being "driven out" becomes. This gives support to the belief of the person performing the ritual, that they are indeed working with a strong, negative power. They will then need to make an extra effort to dislodge the disturbing energy. And so the cycle continues.

Assuming the ritual is successful and the demon has been driven out, what becomes then of the demon? It has been given reality by the person performing the ritual, possibly also by the person from whom this energy has been "driven." So now we have an energy that has been empowered wandering around looking for another host. That does not sound like a win-win situation to me.

The very words "driving out" imply there actually is something to drive out. The belief that there is something there, and it is in any way "evil" is a product of our lack of understanding or our refusal to face the shadow within.

If any charge or information, no matter what name you give it, falls within your ability, meaning that your heart is open enough for it to embrace the charge that is presenting, then that charge will be effortlessly absorbed into the greater awareness of who you are. Contrary to the fears of many, it will not take possession of you but will become one with you. It is only fear, mostly just fear of the unknown, that allows any information to have power over you. As the unknown becomes known, the fear levels drop accordingly.

If, instead of seeing a negative manifestation as the work of the devil or some demon trying to possess someone, we see it as charge expressing itself as it seeks balance, then I believe we are on track to significantly reduce any manifestations on the planet today that we may call evil. It would help if there were a lot more people practicing this. The more people who can embrace this energy, the less it will manifest, the easier it becomes for those who follow.

Seeing energy, manifest or unmanifest, as information seeking balance is such a different approach to life's "problems" that it is unlikely to catch on quickly. Yet, when you can personally experience the benefits of approaching life this way, you will truly wonder why it took so long to come to that point. It is so simple, so powerful, so profound, and the more you practice it, the easier it gets. By developing an open, fearless heart, memory held as shadow can be embraced and the charge released, thus empowering everyone concerned.

Demons, devil, goblins, gremlins, and gargoyles—people have such amazing ways of picturing the dark side. Assuming the records we have available are a true and accurate representation of history—a big assumption—mankind has created many ways of portraying evil. It has created many ways of portraying good as well, the need to polarize being a product of a lost mind trying to find itself.

Different cultures have different demons—for some, one is enough, while others need a multitude, one for each day of the week. I do not think that the externalization of our dark side was without reason. Accepting that we are lost within the drama, we could not have understood human nature, if we did not have something outside of us by which to gauge our own state of being. We needed a mirror to reflect back to us and show us who we were/are. When humanity got lost in the mirror instead of using the mirror to help understand itself, it became the experience instead of the one witnessing the experience, and it took a step away from understanding its true nature. Alice in Wonderland indeed.

But externalizing the dark side is not without value. It enables us to use the information to see which aspects of the dark side, which demons, most trouble us. Which ones control us? And which ones do we not notice at all? There is a lot more value to this approach than most imagine. To understand this better, we need to go on a journey beyond death's door. Before we can go on this journey, we need to acknowledge, even if only temporarily, that we have a soul. For what else can be the witness to the journey? If you believe yourself to be just the body that dies, then there can be nothing for you after the physical body is dead. Some believe this, but most prefer not to.

Exercise

At first, many of the exercises that you've found at the end of the chapters may seem difficult. It is, after all, a new way of being for many of us. With frequent practice, the concept that feelings are not ours will become second nature allowing you the safety to feel more than you have ever done before.

For this exercise, try putting your self in the shoes of another, imagine how they are feeling, and why are they different from you. Their past has created their present, who are we to judge the past of another. Are their feelings any less important than yours? Are they less real simply because they may be different from yours?

I recall someone recently saying that we cannot be connected to each other. If we were, we would think the thoughts and feel the pain and joy of everyone, which would, of course, be overwhelming. It would only be too much, however, if you took all of those thoughts and feelings personally.

Enlightenment, self-realization, omniscience, omnipresence, omnipotence all indicate that we are indeed all connected, in some way. As we learn to not take personally all we think and feel, so we take a step closer to our personal enlightenment.

Whenever you notice a feeling arising, simply acknowledge the feeling, allow it, but try not to get lost in it. Soon your shadow self will be safely accepted, and you can begin to create a world in a more conscious loving way.

Chapter Thirteen
Changing Your Reality

The soul forgets its true nature, accepting completely the identity of the baby. Within the given framework, the body, the personality, the time and place of birth, the social customs and expectations, the child develops. Having lost itself in the drama, the tendency is to take the drama very seriously. And this results in judgment, likes and dislikes, preferences. As the child further develops the ability to personalize its experience, so it learns to be more judgmental.

Shadow forms, and denial becomes a skill that the child uses to survive what it perceives as a difficult or hostile world. The shadow aspects are reinforced by a society that knows no different. The child learns to become more skillful at denial and hiding the shadow away. As the dark side is denied, charge builds. We have already seen how any denied aspects of self can manifest as either internal imbalance, dis-ease, or external conflict. By burying our shadow even deeper out of shame or fear, we are creating an even greater inner imbalance. All charge is doing is simply attempting to find balance. On a very basic level, that which is not loved is seeking to be loved. Who we are is adding to the current worldview, and the more we love ourselves, the more our environment will reflect that back to us. The more we fail to love ourselves, the more the environment will reflect that back to us as well.

Within our current worldview, we struggle to make a happy life for ourselves and our families. We do all we can, but where we have failed to love a part of ourself, we tend to quickly go into blame, which adds fuel to the fires of discontent that are already burning brightly. This has the effect of increasing the feeling that we need to do something to control our environment, to make it safe for ourselves and our families. When this feeling leads us down a path that attempts to create safety at the expense of the safety of others, we are entering the world of global insecurity.

Now at the least, they are convinced that all of their problems are caused by other people's selfishness and unfairness, even if they weren't sure before. In all fairness, there might still be a part deep inside where they know this is not the case, but the opinion of the majority rules, and, afraid of going against the stream, they allow themselves to be carried with the consensus belief. This adds more energy to the manifesting imbalance, which then, of course, requires even more energy to "stabilize" it.

And all the while charge builds.

The real importance of this, I believe, is that if the charge of the shadow has not been released prior to the moment of death, then the remaining charge and all belief patterns, hopes, and desires will survive the death of the physical and play an important part in the next steps of the journey of the soul.

We meet, on a daily basis, much of who we are. We meet our shadow side, we meet our loved side, and everything in between. The key to who we will meet tomorrow is in how we deal with who and what we meet today.

I was introduced recently to the work of Constantine Cavafy, a little know Greek poet who died in 1933 and this poem, "Ithaca," so wonderfully describes the journey that I want to include it now.

Ithaca

When you set out on your journey to Ithaca,
pray that the road is long,
full of adventure, full of knowledge.
The Lestrygonians and the Cyclops,
the angry Poseidon – do not fear them:
You will never find such as these on your path,
if your thoughts remain lofty, if a fine
emotion touches your spirit and your body.
The Lestrygonians and the Cyclops,
the fierce Poseidon you will never encounter,
if you do not carry them within your soul,
if your soul does not set them up before you.

Pray that the road is long.
That the summer mornings are many, when,
with such pleasure, with such joy
you will enter ports seen for the first time;
stop at Phoenician markets,
and purchase fine merchandise,
mother-of-pearl and coral, amber and ebony,
and sensual perfumes of all kinds,
as many sensual perfumes as you can;

visit many Egyptian cities,
to learn and learn from scholars.

Always keep Ithaca in your mind.
To arrive there is your ultimate goal.
But do not hurry the voyage at all.
It is better to let it last for many years;
and to anchor at the island when you are old,
rich with all you have gained on the way,
not expecting that Ithaca will offer you riches.

Ithaca has given you the beautiful voyage.
Without her you would have never set out on the road.
She has nothing more to give you.
And if you find her poor, Ithaca has not deceived you.
Wise as you have become, with so much experience,
you must already have understood what Ithaca means.

Constantine Cavafy, 1911

Cavafy's use of the Lestrygonians and the Cyclops, and the angry Poseidon to represent the demons along the way is a wonderful explanation of the externalization of our shadow. Do not fear them, you will not encounter them on the path if you do not carry them within your soul. We can see from his writing, how, if the shadow of the Lestrygonians, the Cyclops, and the angry Poseidon still has a place in us, unhealed and denied, we will meet those aspects of self along the road.

The overall message is to enjoy the journey; it is not the goal that counts but what happens along the way. The poem urges us to have as pleasant a journey as possible with less importance placed upon the goal.

To guarantee that we will not meet our demons on the road, we need to release the charge we hold around these unloved parts of our self. If we fail to embrace the shadow while we are alive, there will be no one to do it when we are dead. This does not necessarily mean that the information remaining after death will just disappear in a puff of smoke.

I think it can be likened to a sailing ship. Whilst we are alive, we believe ourselves to be in charge, deciding upon a course to follow, where and when to stop, who we take with us on our journey. We do have a lot of choice—we can set the sails to go almost anywhere, though most prefer smooth sailing.

Yet we are not quite as free as we may have thought, as we are still reliant upon the sailing ship itself as a means of transport, and the winds and the tides do influence our decisions. But we have our hand on the helm and that makes us feel good. Remember the soul. It has not gone away while we have been sailing through life, but it remains the constant observer whilst we have become the experience itself. When the physical body dies, as it must ultimately do, who then is in charge of the helm? Who will steer the ship? You may think that the ship went down with you when you died, but the ship is the sum total of all your experiences, all your hopes and your fears, your light side and your dark side, your hopes and your expectations. With no one to hold a course anymore, it becomes the victim of the winds and tides. The ship, being a product of the thoughts and beliefs you held up to the moment of death, is now a victim to those beliefs, to the charge of the shadow still held but not expressed.

The charge seeks balance, but there is no way it can express itself anymore. The charge may manifest in the astral world, sometimes called the 4th dimension but it can find no release until it returns to the third dimension in another physical body. This remaining charge can be a real problem.

According to the Tibetan Buddhists, there is a state where the true nature of mind resides, also referred to as The Dawning of the Ground Luminosity. Those same beliefs hold that the moment of death of the physical is the best opportunity one has to recognize and remain in the true nature of mind. Recognizing and remaining within the true nature of mind would be the goal of many Buddhists, for when the soul is able to rest in the true nature of mind, it signifies an end to the journey of ignorance. An end to being caught in the cycle of becoming, of birth, old age, death and rebirth. It is liberation. Whether this is true or not, I do not know, but the reasoning behind it, and the benefits from practicing awareness of this state are many and immediate. You will not have to wait till you die to experience heaven....

You may also find that just by contemplating the possibility that the true nature of mind exists, you find another reason to work on embracing your dark side while you have a body to do it with.

According to the teachings, even noticing the true nature of mind upon the death of the body is no easy task. In fact, if the teachings are correct, it is almost impossible, especially for those with no training in what to look for. It is believed that when a person dies, the charge, the shadow, the beliefs remain and can be so strong that they propel the awareness, which we can loosely refer to as the soul, through the true nature of mind. This happens so quickly that it does not allow the awareness to recognize the true nature of mind. Instead, the consciousness takes over at the moment of death, as there is no longer a physical body affecting the process, so that the raw concepts and emotional energy have free rein. If the person dying has any deeply held expectations of what to expect following death of the body, they may manifest for that person. Those expectations may include concepts of heaven, hell, and anywhere in between. The fears and desires still held at the moment of death can be so strong that they actually form a "reality," which the person—still identifying beyond death with the body or personality—creates and believes to be real.

Individually, we are complex beings with many hopes and expectations, many fears and desires, many personal judgments. To imagine the singularity that is the body and its associated personality going to one place after death is very hard to imagine. This is where the concept of the soul comes to the rescue. The soul is not bound by the body or personality, in fact, it is likely that the body and the personality are expressions of the soul, not the other way round. If the soul is not bound by the physical form, it may be that it is quite boundless; it may also be that the soul is not limited to any one body at any one time. This gives rise to the possibility of the idea of a group soul. One soul manifesting in many bodies simultaneously.

In his book *Ultimate Journey*, Robert Monroe spoke of many out-of-body experiences. One particular experience related to a man whose desire for a particular woman had drawn that man to the woman's apartment after his death. It was his desire, an emotional charge, which had not been worked out while the man was alive, that drew him to this woman. Monroe was able to convince the man that he had died and needed to move on. In Monroe's words, to level 27, a clearing house, if you will, for lost souls. Having spent a lot of time exploring non-physical realities, Monroe took the man's hand, left, and re-appeared at the clearing house, minus the other man!

Although Monroe did not say this, it is my belief that in order to get to level 27 one must pass through the astral world, or the realm where thoughts and emotions are made manifest. This may not be a truly accurate description, it may be better to say, pass through the formless void, from which all is made manifest. This may require some more explanation, which I will attempt shortly. Passing through this great formless void, en route to level 27, thoughts and emotions that are still held in the awareness of the "soul" as charge are expressed and will immediately manifest.

In his after-death state, our man had little or no control over any charge that he still held and was very much a victim to that charge. Whilst he lived, he may or may not have managed some control over these feelings, but the opportunity to work the charge out existed. As he now passed through the formless void, his desires created his reality. Monroe recalls the man not being with him upon arrival at level 27. Instead, the high charge of sexual desire had manifested a reality of thousands of naked writhing bodies, all trying to have sex. Without any control, the energy of the man had created this reality or had drawn this reality to him by his own unresolved charge. Remember what we were talking about earlier, as all energy seeking balance. All that happened here was a charge that was seeking to discharge, but being without a physical body, it was unable to find balance. Instead the charge expressed itself by creating or discovering a manifestation of the unfulfilled desire.

I think it is unlikely that the entire "soul" that was identified as this man was caught up in an expression of unfulfilled sexual desire during his lifetime. It is more likely that it was just an aspect of his soul—a tiny part of the soul that identified with the charge held at the moment of death, fragmented and sought balance. This would help to explain the term "soul retrieval"—bringing all parts of the soul home, uniting them once again.

This man had not dealt with one of his demons, although he had probably met this demon many times on his personal road to Ithaca. Failing to embrace this shadow aspect of the self and thereby discharge the energy before death, he met the demon of sexual desire after death and was consumed and lost to the charge. Had he recognized this during his lifetime and consciously worked on releasing the charge, on rewiring the brain so that he was no longer a victim to old conditioning, he may still have enjoyed sexual union but would not have been a victim to that desire. He would no longer have projected that charge of desire into the astral plane or the formless void and may never have needed the services of the clearing house for lost souls. Had all charge, all desire, all concepts been released prior to death of the physical, that being may have been able to recognize the true nature of mind following death of the body and remained there.

The big question is, of course, why would anyone want to remain in the true nature of mind when there is so much to do when you have a body? The issue here, I believe, is the difference between having a body with an awareness that is almost completely asleep and an awareness that is wide awake. And thus having the choice to be born or not to be born, instead of always being a product of an unconscious past and being propelled into another body.

According to the Buddhist teachings, missing the true nature of mind after death—whatever the reason— guarantees another birth. Depending upon the intensity of the charge, any charge or desire still held at death will cloud awareness of the true nature of mind, and the charge will seek to express itself. The parts of the soul that still identify with any emotion, concept, or shadow will gradually coalesce and create a mental body, which will eventually be reborn.

I think that the charge held in the shadow at the moment of death plays a part in determining any future manifestation of that aspect of soul in the physical world. Seen simply as a charge seeking to express itself, the nucleus or the soul gathers energy around it—energy that is associated with the various charges it carries—until it is reborn and gets an opportunity to work out the charges. Unfortunately, passing into the body equals a loss of memory, so as we get lost in the body and the personality, we start all over again.

If, as I believe, there are sufficient moments of realization into the true nature of who we are in every lifetime, that manifestation of soul has an opportunity to begin to consciously work through charge. This would require the person to make a start on the rewiring work required of old neural networks, possibly established over many manifestations, and to begin practicing responding to situations instead of reacting to them. Who knows how much progress a person attempting this for the first time would make? But by looking for answers within instead of externalizing all the time, each step back toward a greater knowing would be a step toward defeating the hold the shadow has over the individual and a step toward greater freedom and self-empowerment.

As any manifesting aspect of soul, which we refer to as a person, begins to consciously rewire the brain, open the heart, and bring the dark side into consciousness, any charge they carry is reduced. When death comes, carrying or identifying with less charge than before, the soul does not fragment so much and there is less charge that seeks balance. Still the soul misses the true nature of mind, it still has desire, and "unfinished" business. But, as there is less charge than before, so the coalescing energy drawn to the soul is less dense or intense than before. This results in a new birth with an awareness that has already done a lot of work rewiring the neurons and opening the heart. And the journey "home" has well and truly begun. Eventually there is no charge, or fear, or shadow, or desire that will prevent the soul from seeing and resting in the true nature of mind.

At that moment, I believe, we have regained the ability to choose whether to return to the physical world or not. Prior to resting in the true nature of mind, we remained victims to our past. Any attachment or identification with the past creates a future, we can only work to create another body, another personality, another future, within the framework created out of the past. We cannot find any true personal freedom whilst we associate with our past. So we truly are products of our past, and if that past has been to deny the shadow, then that is who we will become.

To recap all this as simply as I can: Starting from birth the baby loses itself in the drama; it takes the drama seriously and personally. Charge is created through a lack of awareness, a seemingly inherent part of human nature. The person fails to let the charge go before death, again due to a lack of awareness and strong association with the personality. As intense charge, memory is carried by the soul through the true nature of mind, giving the soul no time to even realize it has passed through the true nature of mind. The body falls away, and all that is left is memory, beliefs, and the charge of the shadow self. The sum total of the memories, concepts, and charge will meet with the demons of fears still held and unresolved backpack issues. The person may not have met the Lestrygonians on the physical road, but the road does not stop when the body dies.

There is no longer a body, and the charge is lost in space, seeking some way to balance itself out. It can only do this by entering another body, being born, and—wouldn't you know—once again forgetting all of the above.

It might help to understand that the true nature of mind is here, now, always has been, and always will be. It is not waiting for you to die before it shows itself.

It might also help to know that the formless void—that from which all is created and to which all returns—is not confined to some other realm. Though we can refer to an aspect of this formless void as the astral world, really the void is everywhere, all of the time. The formless void could also be called the cosmic soup we spoke about earlier, the sea of consciousness in which we all swim. It may also be called the mind—of god if you like—the non-local mind, but not whatever you think your personal mind to be.

Whoever we believe ourselves to be, light and dark, we are in the same sea of consciousness as everyone else. Who we are—every single one of us—is energetically transmitted out from us into the sea from where it manifests.

As Chogyam Trungpa Rinpoche has said, "Since all things are naked, clear and free from obscuration, there is nothing to attain or realize. The everyday practice is simply to develop a complete acceptance and openness to all situations and emotions. And to all people—experiencing everything totally without reservations and blockages, so that one never withdraws or centralizes into oneself."

Like life itself, this book is all about the journey. There are as many different paths as there are people. The journey that Chogyam Trungpa Rinpoche describes above is both very simple and very difficult. I believe these words will not appear in our lives until we are ready to try and understand what they mean. Practice will only arise from a readiness to explore the meaning. Yet this small quote is too big for many to really understand when they first hear it. It raises too many questions and doubts in the questioning, intellectual mind. So we build a bridge, from our old, "safe" knowing, into a new land, and because life is a journey waiting to be explored, we begin to cross the bridge.

It doesn't matter whether you believe in the shadow or not. It is just a word used to describe a part of who we are. It doesn't matter whether you believe that you have a soul or not, if you believe in a god or not. It is not important what you think about the true nature of mind, about reincarnation or even that we may all be one in consciousness.

What does matter is that you believe in yourself, that you believe you can make a difference. There are many ways to make a difference, some of them loving and supportive of self and others, some destructive and thoughtless of others. You can only be led by your conscience. We all appear to be subject to the collective view of the world, and we are all responsible for that collective view. Where you may disagree with the collective view, where you meet it head on, when you harbor anger, or hatred, or any lack of love in your heart, it will produce results. Every action does. But will these results create a win-win situation? Will they give you the peace you seek? Perhaps in one area of your life you will feel victorious or defeated, but tomorrow brings that same challenge only from a different place.

The next time you feel yourself being drawn into fighting an injustice, try another way. Before you raise your voice in anger, stop for a moment, think, and ask yourself, "What is this thought doing to my body? What chemicals am I making when I have this thought? Are these chemicals good for me? Are they contributing to future health issues? Would I wish these chemicals on my loved ones?"

And then ask yourself, whether your anger, your judgment are really going to help change the situation? Are they going to make a positive difference to the world? Perhaps there is a way to make a positive difference without poisoning yourself. Many people who are coming from a place of humility and compassion are making a big difference every day. That they are needed in today's world is obvious. Someone has to love the manifesting dark side.

That there is a need for these people is a sign that the world has not really changed very much throughout history. A sign that, after many wars, revolutions, resistance, change, legislation, coups, marches for peace, injustice is still there just as it always was.

Are we truly any better off now than we were thousands of years ago? Many of us may have electricity, water coming into our homes, cars, roads, airplanes, computers, but are we any better off? Are we more civilized? Or less? Have we evolved beyond the need to achieve our deepest needs without recourse to war? Obviously not. Are we able to settle disputes without anger? Obviously not. Have we created a society that is fair and just for all? Obviously not.

Fortunately, there are people who strive to make this a safer, happier world for everyone, but there have been people doing that for a very long time. What emotions dominate in much of the world today? Even those living in the so-called peace and comfort of the West live with fear just behind the curtain. Fear for their children, for their jobs, for their possessions, for their health, for their liberty, for their lives. Is this a sign of a civilized society? This fear is not limited to any one country. It is a global epidemic.

As our own past creates our current reality, so it does for the collective. Unless we are able to step out, even for just a moment, from the shadow of the collective, we will not see this clearly. If we cannot see clearly what is happening, how our worldview is created, then we will forever remain powerless to bring about change. As mentioned earlier, the current manifesting reality is so intense, has so much power, is so real that we feel compelled to do something about it.

And yet, all the doing in the history of the world has simply kept us stuck in an eternal repetition of the past. We still try and fix problems in the same old way. And we come up with the same old solutions to the same old problems.

Unless we are able to come up with a very different approach, the problems will still be here tomorrow, will still be here in 100 years time, and we will still be trying to fix them in the same old ways.

Maybe this is all that life is about. Fall into a drama somewhere in time and space, play the part well, maybe get an Oscar, die, the curtain falls for you, and it's all over. Interesting, but I think most of us would prefer that there were more meaning to our being here than that. Perhaps, though, that is all there is to life—the play of interacting forces and emotions. It may not be up to anyone to "solve" the problems of the world, simply to learn ways and means of dealing with life's situations and surviving as best they can. We come, we do what we do, and we leave. Nothing to fix, nothing to do, nothing to save. We pick our ground, we make a stand, we leave behind the results of lives for other generations to do with what they can.

My intuitive knowing tells me there is more to life than that, but where did my intuitive knowing come from, and why was I blessed with it? I have offered some attempts to explain this, but I do not really know the answer, and perhaps I never will. Perhaps there is no answer, perhaps it is all random. Unlikely, but an open mind must accept the possibility.

There is an old saying, "Life is what we make it." How very true! I believe the time is close for a major overhaul in what we are making, what we have made in the past is not what many want to make in the future. There is a large groundswell calling for change, and many different avenues are being explored—many trying to work the current reality and some going beyond the confines of previous experience, everything is possible. Many certainly believe that we are on the threshold of major change.

The dilemma is how can we manifest that change. What does that new reality look like? We are caught with one foot in the past and the other poised, looking for a future. If we knew where that future lay, we could place our foot with some certainty. Unfortunately, we cannot imagine that future because we have no reference, nothing to guide us. We have not been there before and, consequently, we have to explore options from the known, the familiar ground that we have been "comfortable" in for millennia. The problem there, of course, is that, whilst we are basing our future on our past, we will still struggle within the paradigm that created the past. Out of the past will come our future, yet if we are serious about a new future for ourselves, then we need to stop projecting our current thinking into our future, as it will just create more of the same.

What to do? The past is the past, we don't think we can change that, although some scientists are questioning that. How can we make any fundamental changes, given that we appear to be locked into reacting to the effects of our past.

I remember hearing a story once, about a man who went in search of his teacher. He traveled for many years until, eventually, he found the person he was looking for. This person sent our man away, with no words, no expectations. For many more years, the man wandered, trying to make himself worthy of his teacher. After some time, he returned to the teacher but was once again turned away. Now, more than ever, he realized the reason he was being sent away. He could not see his teacher because his vision was obscured by his own personality, his expectations. In his subsequent wanderings, he used every situation he was confronted with to look at himself and his reactions. Slowly, he was able to let go of his old way of seeing, his old expectations, until one day, returning to the house of the teacher, he found the door open and the room empty. He had come home to discover that he was the teacher he had been looking for. Some people would say that he was working through his karma.

Yet without traveling the path with some awareness, he could never have reached this understanding. I guess the moral of this story is that we can seek forever, but until we turn our gaze inward, we can never find what we are looking for.

Exercise

Think about your own journey to Ithaca.

Author's Note

If I have misquoted anyone it is not intentional and should be seen for what it is—the fallibility of human nature. It is not a deliberate attempt to mislead or confuse. So if you have been misquoted, please accept my apologies now.

www.ingramcontent.com/pod-product-compliance
Lightning Source LLC
Chambersburg PA
CBHW022016090426
42739CB00006BA/163